ISBN 978-1-905184-32-3

This picture of Class 4F No. 44135 from 22A Bristol was taken at Haresfield on 18th August 1951. Haresfield is between Gloucester and Standish Junction where the old Midland and GWR lines ran parallel. The train is seen on the Down Midland line with the Up line to the left. The Up and Down GWR lines, Cheltenham and Gloucester, are seen to the right. The train was a Class D semi-fitted express freight train, that particular class of train requiring at least one third of the wagons to be equipped with the vacuum brake and to be connected to the engine.

COLLECTION R. J. ESSERY

EDITORIAL

Those readers of *Midland Record* who also take *LMS Journal* will know that in the editorial for *LMS Journal* No. 18 I said that this year's Warley Model Railway Club's annual exhibition, to be held at the National Exhibition Centre, Birmingham on 1st and 2nd December, would be a memorable event, and I am now able to confirm that it will be held in Hall 5, which has 15,000 square metres of space, the largest hall at the NEC.

There will be some 75 working model railway layouts including five from overseas. Of particular interest will be the celebration of the 60th Anniversary of the end of the 'Big Four', focusing on the end of the LMS, promoted by the LMS Society and the *LMS Journal* team. Of course, the end of December 2007 also marks the end of the pregroup era and I understand that pregroup models will also figure at this exhibition.

I will be accompanied by Graham Warburton, but sadly, *Midland Engines/LMS Locomotive Profiles* editor Dave Hunt will not be with us due to his son's wedding taking place on the opening day. For my part I look forward to seeing readers and contributors at what is our annual 'face to face' meeting. Although it is not our practice to announce new titles until they are in the warehouse, I am going to make an exception on this occasion. In addition to some new *LMS Journal* publications, *Midland Record* No. 26 will be launched. I am pleased to say that this will contain the long-awaited article on Washwood Heath marshalling yard, made possible by Mark Norton allowing me to use some of his late father's pictures in this article.

I would like to remind readers who may be planning to visit Warley, perhaps for the first time, that Saturday is always a very busy day, so if you wish to avoid the large crowds, Sunday is a better day to attend the club's 40th anniversary exhibition. I look forward to seeing readers and contributors during this event.

Bob Essery

MIDLAND RECORD

Editor: BOB ESSERY

CONTENTS

Designed by Paul Karau
Printed by Amadeus Press, Cleckheaton

Published by Wild Swan Publications Ltd., 1-3 Hagbourne Road, Didcot, Oxon, OX11 8DP. Tel: 01235 816478.

LMS ex-Midland Railway 5ft 3in Class 3F 0—6—0 No. 3245, stationed at St. Albans, leaving the yard at St. Albans (City) station at 6.10 p.m. on 4th May 1946. When the picture was taken, the train, which ran as a Class H freight through to its destination, was moving at about 4 mph. The photographer recorded 'This was the regular evening departure that ran to Luton but could have gone much further. Unfortunately, I failed to record its destination but I vaguely recall the signalman mentioning Luton. Note the old grounded coach body to the left. Every wagon visible was an oldish wooden-bodied one, mainly 7- or 8-plank mineral wagons'.

E. D. BRUTON

The beauty of the Midland was probably epitomised by a Johnson Single in charge of square-panelled clerestory stock, as seen in this c.1907 photograph of No. 124 with a 2/05 p.m. down Leeds express at Mill Hill. One of the famed '115' Class, 124 was built in February 1899, renumbered 678 in July 1907 and lasted until withdrawal in August 1926.

A. C. ROBERTS

THE JOHNSON BOGIE SINGLES

by DAVID HUNT

LOCOMOTIVE aesthetics is almost by definition a subjective matter and one that is calculated to raise hackles and drive partisans to the barricades, so I hope that my first statement in this article will not alienate too many readers. To many Midland Railway devotees, myself included, the Johnson single wheelers that were built during the latter part of the 19th century were the pinnacle of late Victorian express locomotive styling.[1] Being unashamedly of that persuasion, I have made them something of a pet subject over the years, during which time I have gleaned much information about them. Together with Bob Essery and Fred James, I had hoped to make the engines the subjects of titles in the *Midland Engines* series of books but we have been unable to locate sufficient drawings of each class to ensure the sort of coverage we like to achieve in those works. Consequently, I have prepared this article to give a brief overview of all the Johnson 4–2–2 classes in the hope that it will be of interest to readers and to make available some of the material I have gathered. Having mentioned aesthetics in my opening remarks, I will not refer to the subject too much in this article, although when describing the Bogie Singles it is difficult to avoid it; in any case, my good friend Jack Braithwaite can wax far more lyrical about Johnson's achievements in that field than I ever could!

ORIGINS

By 1866, Matthew Kirtley had abandoned the single driving axle for express passenger locomotives in favour of four-coupled designs but in 1887 S. W. Johnson resurrected the type, albeit with a leading bogie rather than a single pair of carrying wheels, and over the following thirteen years built no less than 95 of them.[2] So why did Johnson revert to an arrangement that had gone out of favour over twenty years earlier? The

simple answer is that he was able to employ two things which Kirtley couldn't – steam sanding and a 17½ ton axle loading. The question of single versus coupled driving wheels, which Kirtley had finally resolved to his own satisfaction when the last of the '30' Class 2–2–2s was built in 1866 and the first of the '156' Class 2–4–0s appeared, was a complex equation of metallurgy, technology, friction and weight distribution. So, before embarking on a description of the Johnson Singles, it will pay to examine briefly some aspects of that argument.

From the earliest days of railways, most locomotive engineers had preferred to use single driving axles rather than coupled wheels wherever possible. The main reasons were simple. Manufacturing costs were lower, maintenance was easier and cheaper, lubrication was simpler and less wasteful, and internal friction was less. The main drawback to a single was its greater propensity to slip because of reduced friction at the rails of one rather than two or more pairs of drivers, but if trains were light the tractive effort required was fairly low and the problem was not seriously limiting.[3] A large proportion of an engine's weight could be placed on the driving wheels without exceeding permissible axle loading and the developed power could be transmitted through one pair of wheels without too much slipping. This made them suitable for the relatively light passenger trains of early years but as the demands of the Traffic Department for speed and haulage capacity increased, locomotives had to be more powerful, which meant them becoming larger and heavier. Not only was it more difficult to absorb the power output via a single pair of driven wheels without slipping, but it was no longer possible to have as large a proportion of the engine's weight resting on them. In the mid-1860s, the standard of the Midland's permanent way meant that

Kirtley was only able to design locomotives with a maximum of about twelve tons on any one axle. Thus, a coupled design was preferred so as to put more of the locomotive's weight onto the driven wheels without exceeding the permissible axle loading and to preserve traction.

On the other side of the coin were the more complex and costly construction of a four-coupled locomotive and the increased internal friction of the moving parts. There were also problems caused by the available materials. Wrought-iron tyres, which were the best Kirtley could employ prior to the early 1860s, were easily distorted by anything more than moderate loads, and the tyres on a particular locomotive were prone quite quickly to wear unevenly. This meant that an engine would end up with coupled wheels of slightly different diameters, introducing strains on the crank pins and side rods that at best set up mechanical resistance and at worst led to bent or broken rods or sheared crank pins. Later experiments suggested that well over twenty percent of the rolling resistance of an iron-tyred, four-coupled locomotive was due to friction in the coupling rods and crank pins. Even if mechanical failure did not occur, the cost of regularly having to machine all the tyres on a locomotive to the diameter of the most badly worn, as well as replacing them when they reached scrapping size, was expensive and time-consuming. Developments in steel technology by Krupp and Borsig in Germany changed things considerably and during the late 1850s it became feasible to produce seamless tyres of crucible or Bessemer steel, the former being the harder. Previous attempts to make steel-faced tyres had not been really successful but the German technology enabled them either to be cast then rolled, or rolled from annuli punched out of steel ingots. Their introduction was a milestone in railway locomotive history and, although uneven wear was never completely eliminated, the overall wear on steel tyres was reduced so much that it ceased to be a major problem.

The Midland Railway began to use experimental steel tyres on some 0–6–0 goods engines in about 1861, the reason for choosing such test beds being that if a tyre failed on a six-coupled engine travelling at slow speed it would probably not lead to a serious accident. Once their worth had been proven on goods engines, Kirtley discontinued the 2–2–2 for express passenger use in favour of his celebrated 2–4–0s with steel tyres. There was still a moderately high degree of friction produced by the side rods, but the tractive advantage of coupled wheels, the relative absence of damaged rods, and the ability to build heavier locomotives without incurring the wrath of the civil engineers over axle loading won the day. As an indication of their greater durability, crucible steel tyres were found to last between 120,000 and 150,000 miles compared with 50,000 to 60,000 for wrought iron. The softer Bessemer steel did not last as long but still gave twice the mileage of iron.[4] As a footnote to the above, towards the close of the 19th century, Ahrons and Rous-Marten noted that some older Kirtley and Johnson locomotives were regularly achieving maximum speeds about 8–10 miles per hour in excess of those at which they had previously been seen running. Ahrons suggested that this may well have been due to reduced friction, not only because of the tensile strength of tyres increasing from 33–35 tons per square inch to 40–45 tons per square inch, but also through newer rails. The introduction in 1896 of 100 pound rails to replace the older 85 pound ones, he surmised, would mean that the rails would be subject to less bending as the locomotive passed over them. Harder steel for both rails and tyres would result in less distortion of both, and all these factors could well have led to a reduction in friction and hence increased speeds.

There was still a feeling among many locomotive engineers, however, that single-driver engines were more suitable for high-speed work than coupled ones because there was, undeniably, less friction due to the fewer bearing surfaces. Patrick Stirling said that a coupled engine, 'Ran like a man wi' his breeks doon,' and favoured the single for express duties. Another worry for locomotive designers was the lubrication and strength of pistons as running speeds increased. To minimise the perceived problem, there was a trend towards using the largest possible driving wheels, thus reducing the number of revolutions and, therefore, piston strokes for a given distance travelled. This kept the maximum piston speed as low as possible and helped set designers' minds at rest. The bigger the driving wheels, however, the more costly they were to produce and the heavier they were, as well as the overall length of a coupled locomotive having to increase to accommodate them. Therefore, the overall cost, size and weight of a locomotive for a given power output could be minimised by omitting one pair of large coupled driving wheels, as well as the side rods, and substituting a pair of relatively light carrying wheels.

The axle loading constraints with which Johnson had to cope had eased considerably since Kirtley's day, and by the mid-1880s he was able to put over seventeen tons on each pair of wheels. Thus, there was the possibility of returning to the single layout with large driving wheels for express passenger engines, but with the heavier trains then coming into service, Johnson was wary of potential problems with adhesion. The old Kirtley singles had suffered badly from slipping, which had caused many delays, and by 1884 Johnson had banned many of them from being used on the main line. Up to that time, sanding of the rails to prevent slipping of driving wheels was by gravity, but wind and the disturbed airflow around a moving engine could prevent much of the sand getting to where it was needed between tyres and rails. This, together with low adhesion weight, was largely responsible for the singles' problems. The District Locomotive Superintendent at Leicester, Robert Weatherburn, had more faith in their abilities, though, and undertook some experiments with one of them. He strengthened the driving wheel springs by adding extra plates, raising the adhesive weight to about seventeen tons, and moved the sand pipes closer to the wheels in an attempt to improve matters. His efforts met with some success and came to Johnson's attention, so when the Derby Works manager, Francis Holt, devised in 1885 a system of blowing the sand to where it could be most effective, Johnson determined to run some more official trials. Holt's first system used the compressed air produced in the Westinghouse pumps fitted to some Midland engines, so Westinghouse-equipped 2–4–0 No. 1309 had it installed, was converted into a 2–2–2 simply by removing its side rods, and had its springs altered to put more weight on the driving wheels. It was then tried over the Settle–Carlisle line and found to perform better as an air-sanded single than it had as a gravity-sanded 2–4–0. A similar exercise was undertaken with one of the Carlisle-based '1562' Class 4–4–0s, again with encouraging results. By this time, the Midland was in the process of becoming an automatic vacuum brake line rather than fitting Westinghouse brakes to all its stock, so Holt redesigned his sanding equipment to use boiler steam instead of compressed air.[5]

With the ability to build locomotives to a higher axle loading and having the means of providing the requisite friction between tyres and rails, Johnson was able to re-consider the single driver as a viable option for express passenger work. Rather than being 2–2–2s, though, the Johnson singles had leading bogies of the type first seen on the Midland with the Kitson 'F' Class 4–4–0s built in 1876 and 1877. The main benefit of a leading bogie was to guide the front of the locomotive into curves more smoothly, not only giving greater stability but also helping to reduce the number of tyre breakages that were relatively common on the leading wheels of locomotives without bogies. The latter problem was thought to be due to the extra strains imposed on large wheels when guiding engines into curves. But

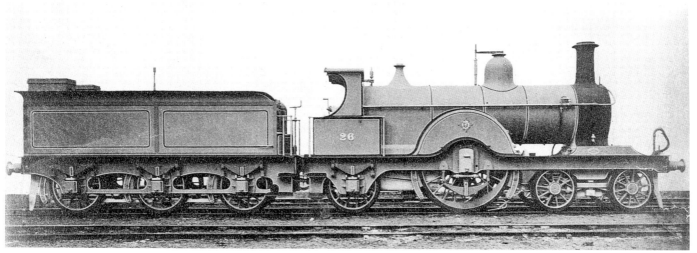

The second Johnson Bogie Single to be built was No. 26, seen here in photographic grey livery and original condition. Only one sandbox was fitted on each side of the engine ahead of the driving wheels whilst the tender had the early toolbox arrangement with two at the rear. This was altered from No. 27 onwards with the rear-mounted boxes omitted and one positioned longitudinally on the front plate at the right-hand side. I don't know when Nos. 25 and 26 were altered to the later arrangement. A close inspection shows the early pattern sand ejectors in which the sand pipes entered at an angle above the steam pipes. Note also the support halfway along the top of the tender for the communication cord that was used to activate the alarm whistle, as well as the absence of lettering on the tank sides and lack of coal rails.   COLLECTION R. J. ESSERY

early attempts at bogie design had missed two vital points; the wheelbase had to be longer than the gauge and there needed to be a measure of side control with a sliding pivot, otherwise instability resulted. It wasn't until Adams patented his design in 1865 that a really successful type of bogie made an appearance in Britain. Johnson had produced his first bogie engine for the Great Eastern just as he left to join the Midland and by January 1876 the 4–4–0 type had been selected for introduction on the Settle Carlisle line. Naturally, therefore, when thoughts turned ten years later to building singles, it was the 4–2–2 that was chosen.

The first of what were eventually 95 Bogie Singles appeared in June 1887 but Johnson recognised that they still had limitations and continued to build 4–4–0s as well in what turned out to be greater numbers than the 4–2–2s. Over the following thirteen years, both types were built side by side with successive batches of each incorporating much the same improvements. In the end, the need for even more powerful, heavier locomotives with larger boilers mitigated against the Singles, steam sanding or not, and the Belpaires, Compounds and Johnson 4–4–0s rebuilt with H boilers won the day. But for sheer elegance and beauty in express passenger engine design, there was never anything in my opinion to equal the

Johnson 4–2–2s. In *The Midland Railway* published in 1953, Hamilton Ellis wrote of them, 'There was something magical about the spectacle of one of these engines at speed'. Having seen the preserved number 673 at Rainhill in 1980, even though it was only travelling slowly, I can understand what he meant. It just seemed to glide along without any fuss or effort.

CONSTRUCTION
It is generally accepted that there were five different series of Bogie Singles, all built at Derby. They were the '25', '1853', '179', '115' and '2601' classes. The '1853s', however, I regard as being more properly divided into two, for reasons that I will explain later, and so I have introduced what I choose to call the '1868' Class.

The '25' Class
The first five Johnson Singles, Nos. 25 to 29, were ordered to O/655 in July 1886 and built at Derby Works between June and August of 1887. Mechanically they were very similar to the '1738' Class 4–4–0s of 1885 but instead of B boilers they carried D class ones pitched 7ft 5½ in from the rails.[6] The barrel of the D boiler was the same as the P boiler, which at 10ft 8⅝ in between tubeplates was 2in shorter than the B boiler with the same 4ft 1in, 4ft 2in and 4ft 3in

diameters outside the first, second and third rings respectively. The three rings were butt joined longitudinally and double riveted to inside and outside joint plates. Transverse joints were lapped and riveted and the middle ring had a strengthening ring riveted to the inside. The firebox wrapper was a single ½ in thick plate that overlapped the third ring and back plate and carried a wrought-iron manhole. Gusset stays were fitted between the doorplate and wrapper, palm stays joined the throatplate to the boiler barrel, and four longitudinal stays joined the top of the doorplate to the front tubeplate with link and pin fixings. Barrel plates and firebox wrapper were ½ in thick Low Moor iron. The 242 brass tubes were 1⅝ in diameter and 11 swg thick at the firebox end, reducing to 12 swg at the smokebox and widened in diameter over the last 4in to 1¹¹⁄₁₆ in to ease the job of removing scale-encrusted tubes through the tubeplate. At the firebox end, 1½ in ferrules were driven into the tubes.

The firebox was the largest so far seen on the Midland at 6ft 6in long with a 19½ sq ft grate and was an inch deeper than that of the B boiler at 5ft 2½ in below the boiler centreline. The inner firebox was ½ in copper with a ¾ in thick copper tubeplate, the foundation ring being wrought-iron. Roof girders were attached to the shell by sling stays, direct stays were 1in thick copper, and the firehole ring was cast-iron. Total heating surface was slightly greater than the B boiler at 1,241 sq ft with the firebox surface 7 sq ft more at 117 sq ft. Together with the large grate, this gave the D boiler a better steam-raising capability, which, added to the increased working pressure of 160 psi, produced a more powerful unit than hitherto.

The regulator was mounted in the dome, which had a copper cover and was fitted with twin gunmetal safety valves having straight levers and brass Salter spring columns. The latter were attached to a single bracket fixed to the middle barrel ring, but because it was below the clothing, they appeared to be independently attached. In addition, there was a single lock-up valve set to 165 psi

mounted on the firebox under a beautifully-shaped brass funnel. Two whistles were mounted on the firebox, the normal one on the centreline and a smaller alarm whistle to the right.

It was the first Midland boiler to have a 'drumhead' smokebox, the front tubeplate being recessed into the barrel rather than attached by an angle-ring and the smokebox having a double wrapper, the inner being the

same diameter as the barrel and the outer one the same as the clothing. This gave the smokebox and boiler a smooth appearance and made the locomotives seem to have even slimmer boilers than before. The elegant 3ft 1in tall Johnson-pattern built-up chimney had a separate liner and a petticoat pipe whilst the smokebox door was the usual dished Johnson pattern with plate hinge and a centre dart fastening.[7]

Water was fed to the boiler by two Gresham & Craven combined injectors and clacks mounted on the firebox backplate, the delivery pipes passing through the firebox water space to the barrel so that the feedwater was pre-heated and too much thermal shock avoided. Lagging was by silicate cotton covered with thin zinc plates that were attached to the boiler and firebox by stools, hoops and crinolines, the whole then covered with thin clothing panels secured by bands and countersunk screws, outside diameter being 4ft 7in. The boiler and smokebox handrail was in one piece that curved elegantly over the smokebox door.

The 18in x 26in cast-iron inside cylinders were bolted to the frames and lubricated by a sight feed displacement lubricator mounted inside the cab front plate, the feed pipe passing through the left-hand boiler handrail and down by the rear of the

No. 26 was photographed at Bedford sometime between 1903, when its lamp iron layout was altered, and June 1907 when it went into Derby Works, from which it emerged as No. 601. Sanding had been applied behind the driving wheels and a one-piece cast-iron chimney fitted, but the small alarm whistle was still mounted on the firebox. The tender had been fitted with coal rails and lettering added to the tank sides and although by this time it had received a front toolbox, the two at the rear were still present, albeit with the lids removed and the tops closed off.
N. THOMPSON

One of the 1889 batch of '25' Class singles, number 1857, is shown in this picture in the mid-1890s with original lamp iron layout and alarm whistle but a replacement one-piece chimney, whilst the tender was still without coal rails but had lettering on the sides. Although the spectacles were lined and there were vees painted on the ends of the spokes, there were no crimson panels on the splasher tops and relatively few embellishments around springs and axleboxes. The front of the guard irons, smokebox hinge and pins were all painted.
COLLECTION R. J. ESSERY

Taken near King's Norton, this photograph of No. 604, ex-29, shows the difference which Deeley's smokeboxes, smokebox doors and parallel-sided chimneys made to the front view of the '25' Class. With the exception of No. 600, these were the only alterations made to the engines after Johnson's time.
COLLECTION R. J. ESSERY

smokebox. Additional lubrication when the engines were drifting with the regulator closed, with no steam to work displacement lubricators, was provided by Furness lubricators at each side of the smokebox near the base. They came in two basic versions, the first type having a more bulbous, onion-shaped body than the later mushroom-shaped one that had a cylindrical oil vessel below the main housing. Drain cocks, operated by linkages from the cab, were provided at the bottom of the steam chest and at both ends of each cylinder. The undersides of the cylinders were probably at first lagged with wood but later silicate cotton was used, both being covered with clothing panels attached to the bottom flanges.

Solid cast-iron pistons were used, each with two cast-iron rings and tail rods. Packing of both piston rods and valve spindles was by conical rings of soft metal, pressed up by spiral steel springs with brass bushes and retaining rings. The rods were lubricated by oil cups bolted to the cast-iron glands and each top slidebar had brass oil cups for lubricating the slidebars and crossheads, which were cast crucible steel. The motion plate was cast-steel with bronze bushed valve spindle guides cast in.

Vertically-mounted bronze slide valves were driven by screw-operated Stephenson link motion, the links and rods of which were case-hardened Yorkshire iron, eccentric pulleys and straps being cast-iron with white metal liners.

Inside frames were 1in thick and made in two sections. The rear portions extended from the drag beam to the rear of the bogie and were spaced 4ft 1½ in apart with the front sections lapped inside and bolted to them. Outside frames were ⅝ in thick whilst buffer and drag beams were 1½ in thick.[8] The driving axle had both inside and outside bearings but the carrying wheels had only outside ones. Outside leaf springs on the driving axle were underhung and inside ones overhung.

All axles were best Yorkshire iron and wheels wrought-iron with 2¾ in thick steel tyres fixed to them by set screws, driving wheels being 7ft 4in diameter when new and carrying wheels 4ft 2½ in on an 8ft 9in wheelbase. The 6ft 0in wheelbase bogie had 3ft 6in diameter wheels and 1⅜ in thick inside frames, which were relieved on the inside faces above the rear horns for clearance from the lower outside slidebars when the bogie was at the limit of its swing. Suspension was by inverted longitu-

dinal leaf springs and equalising beams and the bogie was centred 7ft 0½ in ahead of the driving axle.

Steam sanding was applied ahead of the driving wheels only, with cast-iron sandboxes mounted between the inside and outside frames and early-pattern steam sand ejectors fitted in which the sand pipe entered at an angle above the steam pipe. Steam brakes were fitted with a horizontal actuating cylinder under the ashpan and inside operating rods to beams, hangers and blocks both sides of the driving wheels.

Cabs were typical of Johnson's early styling but with relatively small, rectangular lower sides due to the absence of large driving wheel splashers. They were fairly rudimentary and whilst visually appealing, did little to protect the enginemen. All had automatic vacuum brake apparatus. Weight in working order was given as 43 tons 9 cwt 3 qtr.

Tenders coupled to the '25's when new were 3,250 gallon types first seen with the '1738' Class 4-4-0s. Their tanks were 7ft 1in wide and 3ft 11in deep with a 1ft 4¾ in deep well between the frames and flared coping but no coal rails. By that time it was appreciated that climbing over the top of a tender to reach toolboxes at the rear was hazardous to say the

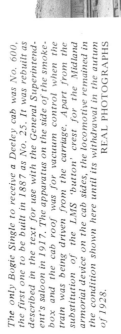

The only Bogie Single to receive a Deeley cab was No. 600, the first one to be built in 1887 as No. 25. It was rebuilt as described in the text for use with the General Superintendent's saloon in 1917. The apparatus on the side of the smokebox and the cab roof was for vacuum control when the train was being driven from the carriage. Apart from the substitution of the LMS 'button' crest for the Midland armorial device on the cab sides, the locomotive remained in the condition shown here until its withdrawal in the autumn of 1928.
REAL PHOTOGRAPHS

No. 600 posed with the General Superintendent's saloon in 1917. The saloon itself was converted from No. 2234, one of the two steam railmotors built for the Morecambe and Heysham line in 1904. It had been rebuilt with a new boiler in 1907 for the Superintendent's use and operated as a self-propelled saloon until being rebuilt again in 1917 without its engine to be paired with No. 600, retaining the number 2234.
COLLECTION R. J. ESSERY

The second series of Bogie Singles differed but little from the '25' Class and it is almost impossible to tell the difference in most photographs except for the number. Apart from the slightly bigger driving and carrying wheels, which do not really stand out, only the fact that they had cast-steel wheels with a more rounded cross-section to the spokes differentiated them externally. No. 1853 was built in February 1889 and sent to the Paris Exhibition where it won the Grand Prix, which is reflected by the commemorative plate in front of the makers' plate on the front framing. It read 'GRAND PRIZE 1889 PARIS EXHIBITION'. The engine was stationed at Kentish Town, where it was painted in the 'London Style' as seen in this late 1890s photograph, with extra lining around the base of the safety valve funnel, spectacle frames, on the axle ends, spring buckle anchorages of the bogie, penultimate top and bottom leaves of trailing and tender springs, and spring buckles. There were double lines to the lower right of the crests and lining on the vacuum hose stand pipe. Its wheel spokes had stripes and vees at the rim and boss; vees were also painted on the tops of trailing wheel and tender axlebox spring hangers and the lining on the axleboxes was extended to the angled faces. It did not, however, have lined red panels on the front portions of the driving wheel splashers. Since being built, the only alterations had been the fitting of a one-piece chimney and the addition of tender coal rails.
COLLECTION R. J. ESSERY

least, and the '25' Class tenders from No. 27 onwards were the first to have toolboxes at the front, one being positioned longitudinally on top of the front plate on the right-hand side.[9] There were also two floor-mounted toolboxes on the front platform in the angles between tank side plates and front plate. A single filler with 'dustbin' lid was fitted in the centre of the tank top at the rear. The one inch thick frames were 5ft 9½ in apart with 7ft 7in wide platforms and the 1½ in thick, 7ft 5in wide buffer beams had curved ends. At the rear, the buffers were self-contained as on the locomotives, but intermediate buffers at the front were controlled by a transverse leaf spring bearing on their backs and connected at the centre to the drawbar. There were long frame slots between the horns with forked spring hangers fitted into rebates at the tops of the slots and bolted on. Footsteps were attached directly to the fronts of the frames.

All five engines went to Kentish Town (numbers 28 and 29 were initially allocated to Nottingham but didn't stay there long) and were an immediate and outstanding success. They were fast, free-running and fairly economical, using fractionally over 0.1 pounds of coal per ton/mile in normal service. Once their initial

evaluation was complete, the decision was taken to carry on building Bogie Singles and O/745 was placed in February 1888 for another five engines. Only three, however, were '25' Class, the other two being slightly different '1853' Class engines that I will discuss later. The three '25's were Nos. 30–32 completed in December 1888. The next order for 4-2-2s, O/796, was for five '25' Class engines Nos. 37 and 1854–1857 but O/809 issued in January 1889 was for five '1853' Class and five '25' Class Nos. 1858–1862. Why locomotives of two slightly different designs were built to the same orders I don't know and even the allocations don't give any clue as the two types were sent to the same sheds. The numbering, of course, followed the then normal practice where Derby Works products filled in gaps rather than being allocated continuous number blocks, which was the case with outside contractor-built engines. As far as I can ascertain, there were no differences between the various batches of locomotives as originally built, eighteen of them eventually being turned out with the last one being No. 1862 completed in January 1890. Replacement chimneys were normally one-piece cast-iron ones.

The '1853' Class

As already stated, the first two '1853' Class engines were part of O/745. Built in February and March 1889, they differed from the '25' Class in only a few details and were supposedly the same weight in working order. Tenders were 3,250 gallon as described for the '25' Class. Numbered 1853 and 34, their cylinders were enlarged to 18½ in, driving wheels to 7ft 6in, and carrying wheels to 4ft 4in. They were also the first Midland locomotives to be built with cast-steel wheels, which had a more rounded cross-section to the spokes and were then fitted to all subsequent Bogie Singles. The remainder of the '1853' Class, Nos. 1863–1867, were built alongside the last '25's as part of O/809 between June 1889 and February 1890 and were the first singles to carry steel boilers, five '1738' Class 4-4-0s and five Kirtley '700' Class 0-6-0s having been fitted with them in 1885 and 1886. Johnson was still wary of steel as a boiler material, though, and ordered that five spare wrought-iron ones be made in case of problems. No. 1853 was specially finished, even to the extent of having all the bolt and rivet heads on its buffer beam and smokebox jacket countersunk unlike the remainder of all but one of the class, and sent to the 1889 Paris exhibition where it

Second of the '1853' Class built was No. 34, which entered traffic in March 1889 and spent most of its time at Bristol with a sojourn at Bedford in the early and mid-1890s. It was photographed at St. Pancras on 18th April 1891 and shows what may be termed the 'standard' livery at that time without the extra embellishments sometimes seen. This is somewhat ironic as the bowler-hatted figure on the footplate bears a strong resemblance to Robert Weatherburn. The engine was in original condition with sanding to the front of the driving wheels only and fitted with an alarm whistle whilst the tender was without coal rails and there was no lettering on the tank sides.

A. C. W. LOWE

What I have chosen to call the '1868' Class is typified in this illustration of No. 1871 taken in about 1904. The deeper frames behind the smoke-box are evident, as are the helical driving wheel springs which replaced the leaf springs of the earlier engines. The locomotive was stationed at Kentish Town, and was recorded by P. C. Dewhurst as being one of Robert Weatherburn's favourites. It is seen here displaying all the hallmarks of Weatherburn's livery treatment as described in the text, including the double line to the lower right of the crest and lining on the vacuum hose stand pipe, and is in immaculate condition. Even the drawhook and couplings seem to have been polished. The underside of the boiler was painted to reflect light onto the polished motion. Normally this was cream and the engines were known as 'yellow bellies', but some of Weatherburn's favourites were recorded by Dewhurst as having white boiler undersides, so it is possible that number 1871 was one of them. The forward of the two oval plates on the front framing is a 'Boiler New' plate fitted when the engine was reboilered in 1902. Built in 1891, it was renumbered 628 in 1907 and passed into LMS ownership, being withdrawn in November 1926.   COLLECTION R. J. ESSERY

won a gold medal. It can't have been easy to countersink ⅝ in rivets into the relatively thin (I think about ⅛ in or ³⁄₁₆ in) plate of the outer smokebox jacket and shows the lengths that the Company was prepared to go to with its exhibition engines. No. 1867 was similarly treated and may have been intended for the Edinburgh exhibition of 1890.

The '1868' Class

The next class of Bogie Singles were built between January 1891 and May 1893 to O/935, O/998, O/1080 and O/1094, the first for five engines and the rest for ten apiece. Although mechanically the same as the '1853' Class, with 18½ in cylinders, 7ft 6in driving wheels, and coupled to the same pattern 3,250 gallon tenders, there were important differences. I have therefore called them the '1868' Class after the first of the type to be constructed in keeping with the system used for other classes, although the Midland never referred to them as such and regarded them as '1853's. Numbered 1868–1872, 8, 122, 20, 145, 24, 33, 35, 36, 38, 39, 4, 16, 17, 94,

97–100, 129, 133, 149 and 170–178, all had iron boilers, the first five being the spares made for Nos. 1863–1867 in case of problems with the steel ones. Their inside frames were deepened between the smokebox and driving wheels and could be seen above the platform, and the boiler was pitched an inch higher at 7ft 6½ in above the rails. Leaf springs on the driving axle were replaced by large double helical springs which, whilst being more 'lively' than leaf springs, have the advantage of being faster acting. On a single-driver locomotive this could be a distinct help for traction and the avoidance of slips. From the '1868' Class onwards, all the remaining Bogie Singles had helical driving wheel springs. The modifications made them nearly three quarters of a ton heavier than their forebears. The first five engines, 1868–1872, had the same sanding arrangement as the '25' Class but the remainder had two more sand boxes and sanding applied both ahead of and behind the driving wheels. Eleven engines, Nos. 1868–1872, 8, 122, 20, 145, 24 and 33, had the same

boiler particulars as the '25' Class but the rest had only 240 tubes, which reduced the total heating surface to 1,233 sq ft. Chimneys were one-piece cast-iron, subsequently used on the remaining Bogie Singles.

The '179' Class

A further five Bogie Singles, Nos. 179–183, were turned out in 1893 with cylinders enlarged to 19in diameter and were the first Midland locomotives to be fitted with piston rather than slide valves. Piston valves were not a new invention – two of Stephenson's Liverpool and Manchester Railway engines had them in 1832 – but although considered more efficient for fast running than slide valves, they had fallen out of favour in the intervening years due mainly to two perceived problems. Lubrication was considered more difficult, and trapped water would damage cylinders as it could not be forced out past piston valves as it could with slide valves. In 1887, W. M. Smith of the North Eastern Railway had developed a system of collapsible segments for piston valves

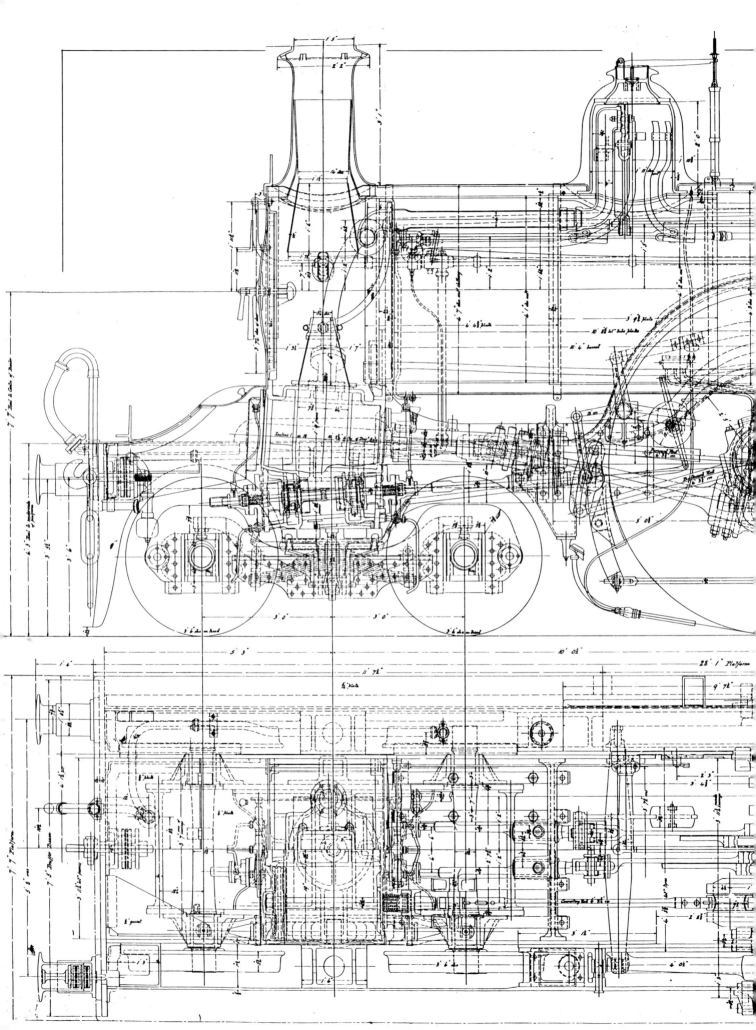

The caption for this drawing appears on page 27.

DRIVING WHEEL 7'-6" DIA   CYLRS 19" × 26"

MIDLAND RAILWAY.
LOCOMOTIVE DEPARTMENT
DERBY.

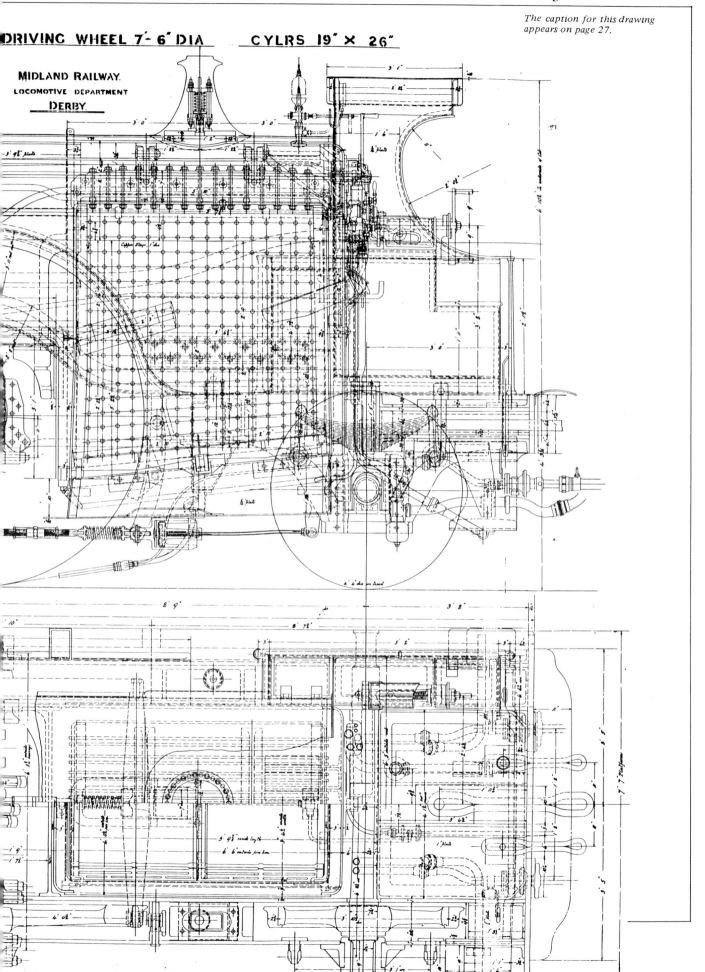

This photograph of '179' Class No. 183 in photographic grey is useful for the amount of detail it shows, such as the steam brake cylinder underneath the firebox, inside helical springs, and tender connections. Note the communication cord stanchion halfway along the tender top.
BRITISH RAILWAYS

The first series of Bogie Singles to have piston valves was the '179' Class built in 1893 and 1896. As can be seen in this photograph of an 1896 engine, No. 76, the higher-pitched boiler and deeper front frames consequent on the fitting of piston valves was immediately obvious. It can be seen that the sand ejectors were to the later pattern in which the sand pipe was in line with the ejector pipe and the steam pipe entered at the side. Also evident is the larger diameter handrail from cab front to rear of the smokebox, through which both displacement lubricator oil pipes passed before running down the rear of the smokebox to the steam chests. The picture was taken between 1903 and 1907 when the engine was allocated to the Birmingham district but its livery showed 'London styling' with lining around the base of the safety valve funnel, cab spectacles, spring buckles, etc. The lining on the ends of the which would relieve the pressure of trapped water. This, together with improvements in lubrication, made them once more feasible in the eyes of several locomotive engineers. As well as improving the steam flow and leading to greater economy, it was claimed that piston valves took less energy to drive them (although the saving probably only amounted to less than half a percent of the power developed in the cylinders) and Johnson reported that they were less prone to wear than equivalent slide valves. The eight inch piston valves on the Johnson Bogie Singles were mounted below the cylinders, which made the design of the steam passages difficult and the engines somewhat less thermally efficient than would have been the case had they been mounted above. Lap was 1⅛ in and lead in full gear ⅛ in.

As well as having the heavier inside frames of the '1868' Class visible between smokebox and drivers, the 179's could he identified by the larger frames above the front platform consequent on the fitting of pis-

ton valves. This also meant that the boiler pitch had to be raised to 7ft 7¼ in from the rails. The first locomotives built still had just one sight feed lubricator, but later ones – I haven't established when the change occurred – had two of them, the oil pipe to the right-hand steam chest running along the top of the handrail pillars and down forward of the left-hand splasher. Later on, the handrail diameter was increased from 1½ in to 1¾ in as far as the rear of the smokebox with both pipes inside it to that point, where they emerged and passed down the front of the barrel. All further piston valve engines had two sight feed lubricators with the later arrangement of oil pipes but the '179' Class was unique in having the Furness lubricators moved from the smokebox sides to the rear of the steam chests. They were also the first to be built with hot-water carriage-warming apparatus, all subsequent engines following suit.

After the first batch of '179's was built, there was a gap of three years before any further Singles appeared

from Derby, then in 1896 another five of the same class were turned out. Numbered 75–79 and 88, their boilers had only 236 tubes, giving 1,205 sq ft total heating surface. They also had the later pattern of sand ejectors where the sand pipe was in line with the ejector pipe and the steam pipe entered at the side. Subsequent singles were built with this feature. Tenders were again 3,250 gallon as described earlier but had coal rails; it is possible that the '1868' Class tenders also had coal rails as built but I haven't been able to confirm it.

The '115' Class

The penultimate series of Bogie Singles are regarded by many connoisseurs as Johnson's styling *pièce de résistance*, particularly the final ten engines which had a slightly different outline to the front framing above the platform. The first five were built to O/1474 of September 1895 and appeared as Nos. 115–119 between November 1896 and March 1897. The '115' Class were basically 4–2–2 ver-

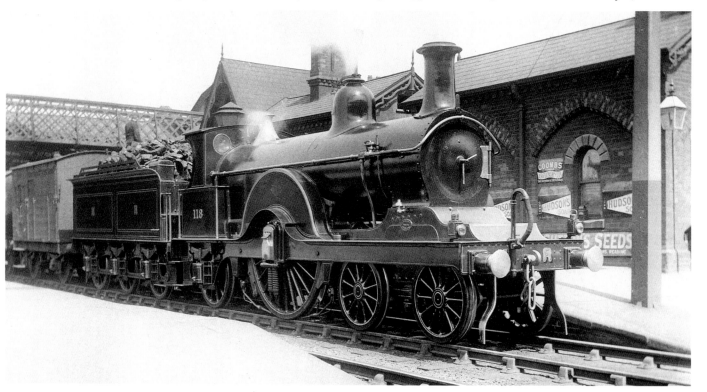

The two batches of '115' Class engines differed slightly in the shapes of their front frames above the platform, some commentators averring that the first series, depicted here by No. 118 at Bedford with an up express in the summer of 1903, were not quite as elegant as the later ones. All had the deeper frames behind the smokebox and curved Salter valve levers with shorter columns evident in this picture. The engine was turned out in what I imagine to have been the average condition of a Bogie Single around the turn of the century, rather than specially prepared for the camera or given particular treatment as someone's favourite. Even so, it is clean and polished with bright metalwork. The lining is 'standard' rather than one of the more florid styles, and in my opinion suits the engine better, too much embellishment seeming to detract from Johnson's superb styling. Note the large rivet in the smokebox door filling the hole where the lamp iron was originally attached.   N. THOMPSON

The second series of '115' Class Bogie Singles had an elegance that was probably unsurpassed. As can be seen in this photograph of No. 120, again taken at Bedford in the summer of 1903, there was a slight difference in frame shape at the front, but apart from 115's cab, the two batches were otherwise identical. N. THOMPSON

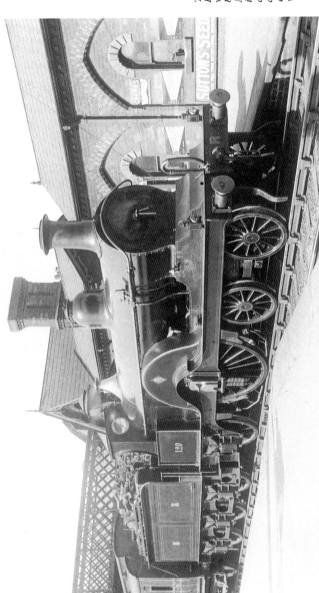

The cab profile on all the '115' Class except No. 115 itself is illustrated in this photograph of No. 124 at St. Pancras in about 1901. As can be seen, the cut-outs met the lower cab side plates further forward than on 115 due to the cab roof being slightly lower.

COLLECTION R. J. ESSERY

No. 115 differed from the rest of its class in the shape of its upper cab. As can be seen from this view, the curve of the cut-outs ended at the rear corners of the lower side plates but on the remainder of the class they met the sides further forward, showing that the cab roof was lower than before. No. 115 was decorated in one of the more florid London area styles with filigree patterns on the cab sides and splashers, which I think was too ornate and detracted from the engine's elegance.

COLLECTION R. J. ESSERY

sions of the '60' Class 4–4–0s with the same 19½ in cylinders, eight inch piston valves and E class boilers pressed to 170 psi. As well as having a higher working pressure, the E boiler was larger than the D, its barrel being two inches longer at 10ft 10⅝ in between tubeplates, i.e., the same as the B boiler. The firebox was 7ft long and 5ft 6½ in deep below the boiler centreline with a 21.3 sq ft grate and 128 sq ft heating surface. The 236 tubes were 1⅝ in diameter and total heating surface was 1,233 sq ft. Other details were as given for the D boiler but they were made from steel, Johnson apparently having decided by then that it could be trusted as a boiler-making material. With deeper fireboxes and piston valves, the boilers were pitched higher than on previous singles at 7ft 10in above the rails and, as a result, the chimneys were only 3ft tall. The Salter safety valve levers, instead of being straight as previously, had a shallow reverse

curve to them and shorter spring columns were fitted.

As a result of the increased boiler length, the frames were two inches longer than the '179' Class and the bogies were moved forward two inches. The bogie wheels and driving wheels were enlarged to 3ft 9½ in and 7ft 9in respectively and the engines were nearly three tons heavier than their predecessors at 47 tons 2 cwt 3 qtr with the springs set to put a notional 18½ tons on the driving axle.[10]* No. 115 differed very slightly from the remainder of the class by having a taller cab, the top of the roof being 11ft 5in above the rails, whereas they were somewhat lower on the remainder although I haven't been able to determine the exact height. The difference is apparent in photographs as the bottom of the curved cut-out on 115 met the lower cabside panel at its rear corner whereas on the remainder the meeting point was a little ahead of it,

leaving a straight portion of the lower cab side to the rear.

The second order for '115's was O/1659 issued in July 1897 and in due course Nos. 120–128, 130 and 131 were turned out from Derby Works between January and April 1899. As already stated, the shape of their front frames was slightly different but the shape of the covers over the frame cut-outs for the cylinders was altered too. The inside frames were also deeper behind the smokebox as could be seen above the platform level. The chimneys on 124 and 127 differed slightly from the remainder as the lips were a little shallower. The mastery of Johnson and his draughtsmen was at its zenith when these engines were designed and they were surely some of the most elegant and visually harmonious creations ever to run on rails.

Tenders for the '115's were originally to have been 3,250 gallons as well, but the order was changed and

* The arrangement of the inside frames differed from those on the earlier engines as instead of having cut-outs for the leading bogie wheels, the front sections were angled inward from a point just forward of the bogie centre, so that at the buffer beam they were 3ft 9½in apart. This allowed for greater strength without limiting the bogie swing and was incorporated in the later '2601' Class as well.

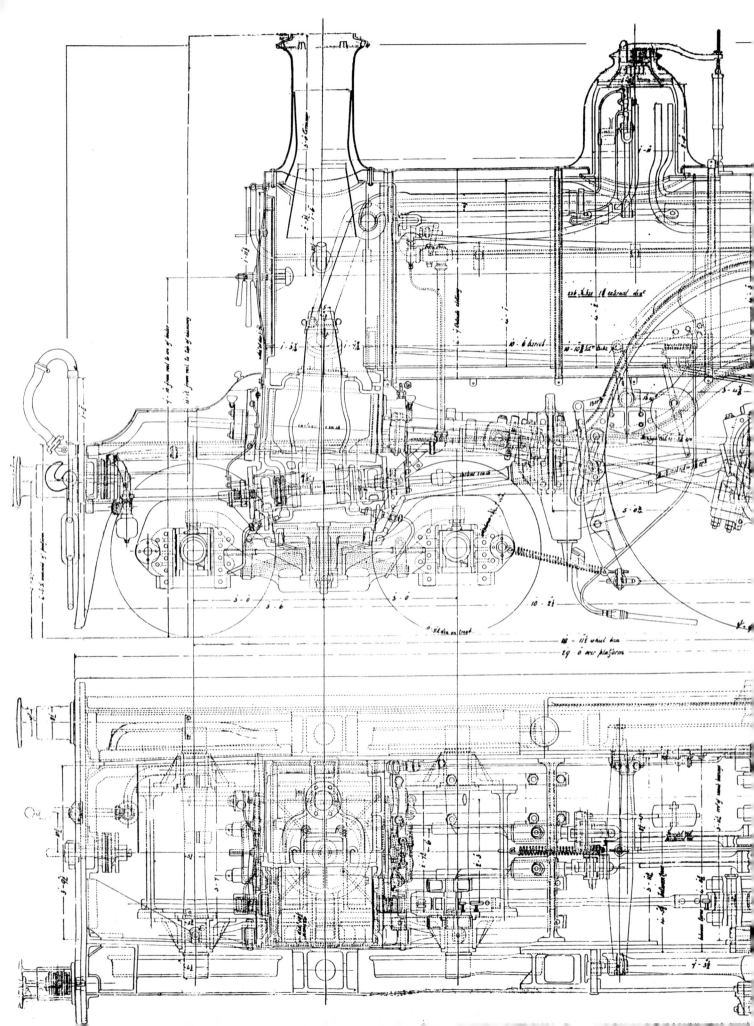

The caption for this drawing appears on page 27.

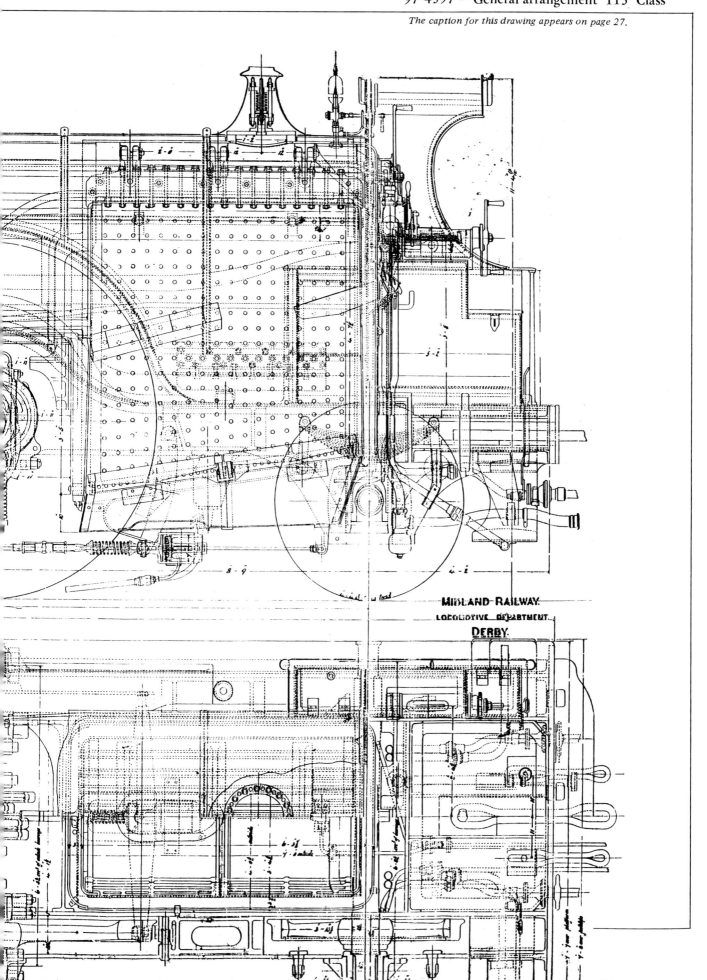

MIDLAND RAILWAY.
LOCOMOTIVE DEPARTMENT.
DERBY.

95-4191 — Smokebox arrangement

*This drawing illustrates the smokebox arrangement and front
elevation of one of the first series of '115' Class engines. It shows
how the chimney liner and petticoat pipe were attached to the
chimney by bolts through spacers between the double smokebox
wrappers as well as why the frames were deeper at the front and the
boiler pitched higher on piston valve engines. It also indicates how
the arrangement of the inside frames differed from that of earlier
engines, there being no cut-outs for the leading bogie wheels as the
front sections were angled inward to allow sufficient bogie swing
without weakening the frames.*

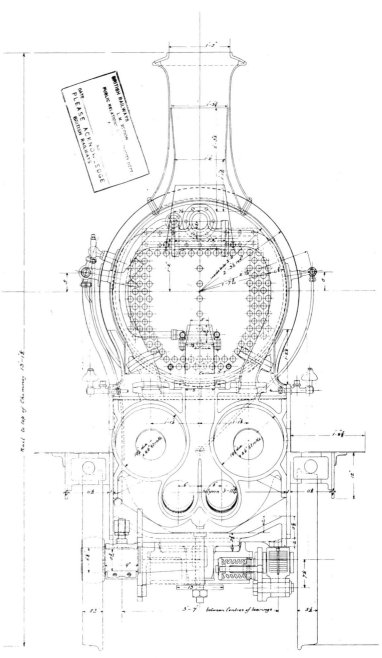

SMOKE BOX ARRANGEMENT

FOR 7'-9" SINGLE ENGINE

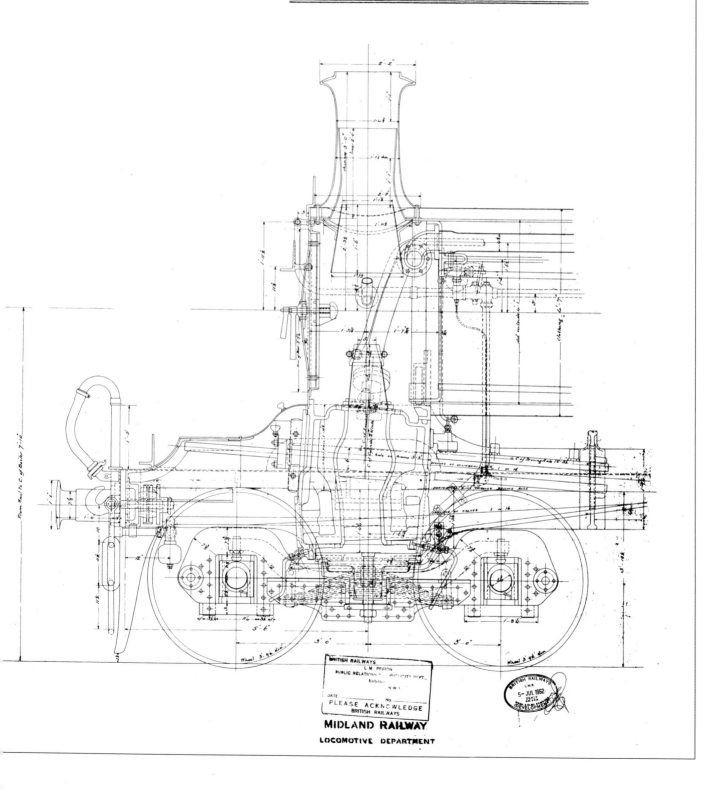

MIDLAND RAILWAY

LOCOMOTIVE DEPARTMENT

Part of drawing 95-4191. The remainder of the drawing and caption appear on pages 24/25.

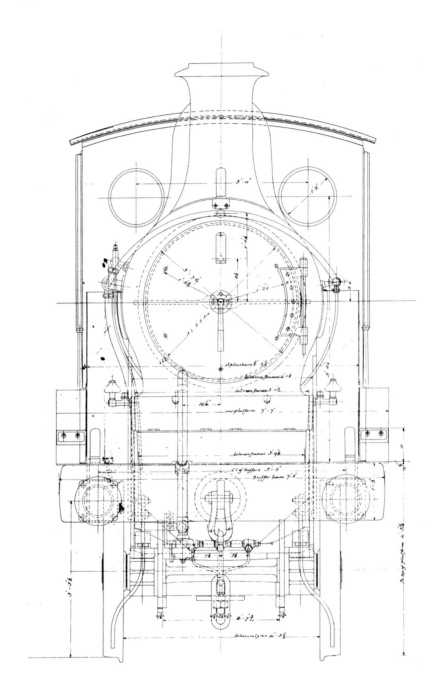

94-4043 – General Arrangement '179' Class
(Drawing on pages 16/17)

This drawing shows the second batch of piston valve engines built in 1896 and numbered 75-79 and 88. As I have written before, the amount of detail incorporated in GAs varied depending on when, where and by whom they were drawn, but those produced by Derby Locomotive Drawing Office were among the better examples. For anyone not used to looking at them, interpretation can be difficult, so although I have more or less included the following notes before, they are offered here to help the uninitiated. Most of the side elevation is as though the engine has been sectioned at the centreline and we are looking through the structure towards the right-hand side, although there are components, such as the cylinders and valves, that are sectioned on different vertical planes. Items such as the springs, bogie equalising beams, platform and splashers on the far side of the engine are shown chain-dotted and some details, such as the boiler tubes, have been omitted for clarity. The plan is in two portions. Above the centreline is a view from above the platform with the boiler and top of the cab removed, although the firebox and some of its cladding are shown. Firebox backplate fittings, which are shown in the side elevation, are not included. Some hidden details below the platform are shown chain-dotted. Below the centreline is a series of sections through components below the platform, but there is no common plane on which they are taken with those through the buffers, driving wheels, cylinders, motion and firebox all being different. Some items, such as the brake rigging, connecting rods and bogie wheels, are not sectioned. Actual construction of the locomotives would have been undertaken using a series of detail and sub-structure arrangement drawings with the overall GA just to illustrate how it all went together.

Points to note include the 'drumhead' smokebox arrangement, with the front tubeplate recessed into the barrel and the double wrapper of the smokebox, as well as the one-piece cast-iron chimney with separate liner and a petticoat pipe. Rather than the water delivery pipe passing right through the boiler to the front ring as on some other Johnson boilers, the one shown here discharged into the second ring just ahead of the driving wheel centreline. The two-piece inside frames with the front sections lapped inside the rear ones to the rear of the bogie can be clearly seen in the plan view. Note that on these engines they were parallel up to the buffer beam.

97-4397 – General arrangement '115' Class
(Drawing on pages 22/23)

Whilst this drawing is supposed to pertain to the first five of the '115' Class, it actually represents only No. 115 in all respects. The depth of the upper cab, and hence the shape at the rear, was peculiar to that engine with the curve of the cut-outs meeting the lower cabside panels at the rear corners, as illustrated in the drawing. The other members of the class had shallower cab tops so that the curves met the lower panels slightly further forward. The front frames had a different profile from those on the final ten engines, as described in the text. The class was the first to have curved Salter safety valve levers with shorter spring columns. Other differences from earlier engines are enumerated in the text but note also the spring from the front brake beam to the rear of the bogie that was added to assist with brake release. Layout and style of the drawing are as described for 94-4043.

Below: *This drawing, No. 01-4970, is described in the Derby Locomotive Drawing Register as 'Special nameplate "Grand Prix" for Paris Exch. Engine'. It was dated 28th February 1901 and the draughtsman was Mathers. It was produced to order number 1926 and the note in the register reads: '4970A. A special size. Larger than standard plate, 4970 not used. Both tracings kept.' This suggests that the original drawing was for a similar but smaller plate, but it was decided that a larger one would be more suitable on this occasion, hence two drawings. The description of the '2601' Class begins on page 29.*

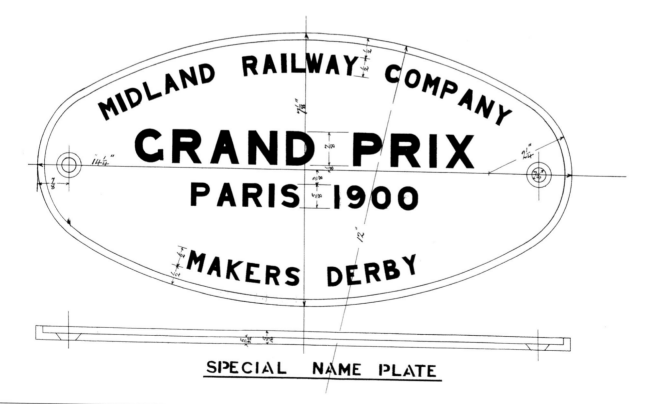

SPECIAL   NAME   PLATE

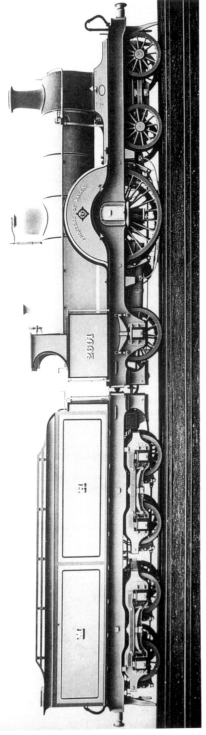

When the '2601' Class bogie tenders were built, the brakes were to the rear of all wheels, as shown in this study of 2601 in photographic grey finish. The picture also illustrates how massive the 'watercarts' were compared with the locomotives.
AUTHOR'S COLLECTION

The first example of the final series of Bogie Singles was exhibited at Paris in 1900 and won the Grand Prix. This picture was taken after its return and it can be seen that the tender bogies had been altered with the frames extended forwards to allow the brakes to be placed ahead of the leading wheels. No. 2601 was one of only two Midland locomotives to be named, the other being 4–4–0 Beatrice, and as is apparent, Princess of Wales had the full Weatherburn treatment and was a 'yellow belly' with cream paint on the underside of the boiler. The maker's plates commemorated the prize and had 'GRAND PRIX PARIS 1900' in the centre. As discussed in the text, some enthusiasts think that the repositioning of the domes and the large bogie tenders spoiled the '2601' Class. I don't. A drawing of the 'Grand Prix' plate appears on page 27.

the first Midland 3,500 gallon ones were produced for them. They differed from later 3,500 gallon tenders as they had 2ft wide, 1ft 11¾ in deep side pockets at the front of the tank so the tank depth was only 4ft 0in instead of the later 4ft 2in, a distinction they shared with the first twenty of the '60' Class 4–4–0s. Otherwise they were closely similar to their 3,250 gallon predecessors, except for self-contained intermediate buffers, and with only an inch difference in height were extremely difficult to distinguish from them.

The '2601' Class

The final group of ten 4–2–2s, built during 1899 and 1900, were not only the biggest of all but were the only ones to be placed in power class 2 after 1906, all the others being in class 1. Their cylinders and valves were the same as those on the '115' Class but they were fitted with 180 psi steel E boilers, only ten of which were ever made and which were the biggest of all Johnson's 'slim' boilers. The barrel was fractionally bigger, being ⅞ in greater diameter and 1/16 in longer than the E boiler, but carried only 228 tubes of 1⅝ in diameter. Diameter over the clothing and outer smokebox wrapper was still 4ft 7in, though. The firebox was a foot longer than that of the E boiler at 8ft as well as being three inches deeper at

5ft 9½ in below the boiler centreline with a 24½ sq ft grate and 147 sq ft heating surface Total heating surface was 1,217 sq ft. Other details were closely similar to the D and E boilers but the dome was moved back to the middle ring and, because of the higher boiler, the chimney was only 2ft 11in tall; like the '115's, they were built with curved Salter valve levers and shorter spring columns.

The large fireboxes meant that the distance between driving and carrying wheels had to be increased by a foot to 9ft 9in and the boiler pitch was raised to 8ft 1in above the rails. Additionally, the platforms were raised 3¾ in to 4ft 6in above the rails and a curved drop portion inserted immediately behind the buffer plank. At this time, Johnson was introducing 3in thick tyres so all the wheel diameters of the '2601's were originally half an inch greater than the '115's.

Apart from their increased length and repositioning of the domes, the most obvious visual difference between the '2601 class' and what had gone before was that they were coupled to massive 4,000 gallon bogie tenders. These were built to increase the distances run between water stops on the main line before the installation of water troughs, and became known as 'water carts'. They were carried on two outside-framed

bogies mounted at 11ft 3in centres and having 3ft 6in diameter wheels 5ft 6in apart. Equalising beams and inverted leaf springs were mounted between front and rear axleboxes on each bogie frame, and all the wheels were braked with brake shoes behind all the wheels. The coal space and tank top could hold about 7 tons of coal. The locomotives were heavier than the previous Bogie Singles and in working order weighed three hundredweight over fifty tons, but even so they were outweighed by their fully loaded tenders.

Some commentators have decried the appearance of the '2601' Class engines for two main reasons: firstly, the repositioning of the dome spoiled the imaginary straight line which joined the tops of the chimney, dome cover, safety valve cover and cab roof on the earlier engines; and secondly, the bogie tenders were too big. Whilst I have already admitted that aesthetics are largely a subjective matter and that 'beauty is in the eye of the beholder', I would take issue with the detractors of Johnson's last Bogie Single design. These engines were actually the biggest of all the Johnson 'slim-boilered' family of all wheel arrangements and represented the last development of the Midland's Victorian style. What followed was the transition phase of Edwardian large-boilered, Belpaire firebox types

No. 21 of the last series was built in 1900 and initially allocated number 2608, but was renumbered before entering service. This picture shows the simpler style of paint scheme applied to these engines without lining on the cab front angle, spectacles, base of safety valve casing, motion bracket, spokes, etc, although there are some additions such as on the spring hangers and leaves. It is of interest that the lining on the cab sides has rounded corners rather than the square type normally seen. The altogether more massive appearance of these engines when compared with the earlier Singles is apparent, as are the altered tender bogies with extended frames and brakes ahead of the leading wheels. BRITISH RAILWAYS

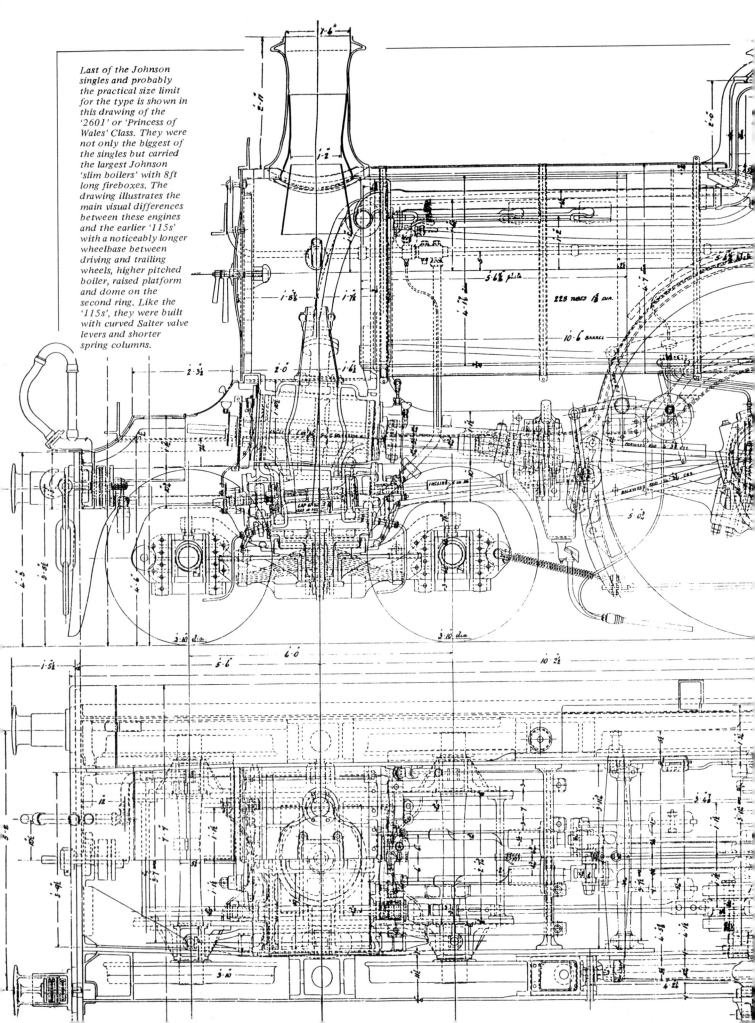

Last of the Johnson
singles and probably
the practical size limit
for the type is shown in
this drawing of the
'2601' or 'Princess of
Wales' Class. They were
not only the biggest of
the singles but carried
the largest Johnson
'slim boilers' with 8ft
long fireboxes. The
drawing illustrates the
main visual differences
between these engines
and the earlier '115s'
with a noticeably longer
wheelbase between
driving and trailing
wheels, higher pitched
boiler, raised platform
and dome on the
second ring. Like the
'115s', they were built
with curved Salter valve
levers and shorter
spring columns.

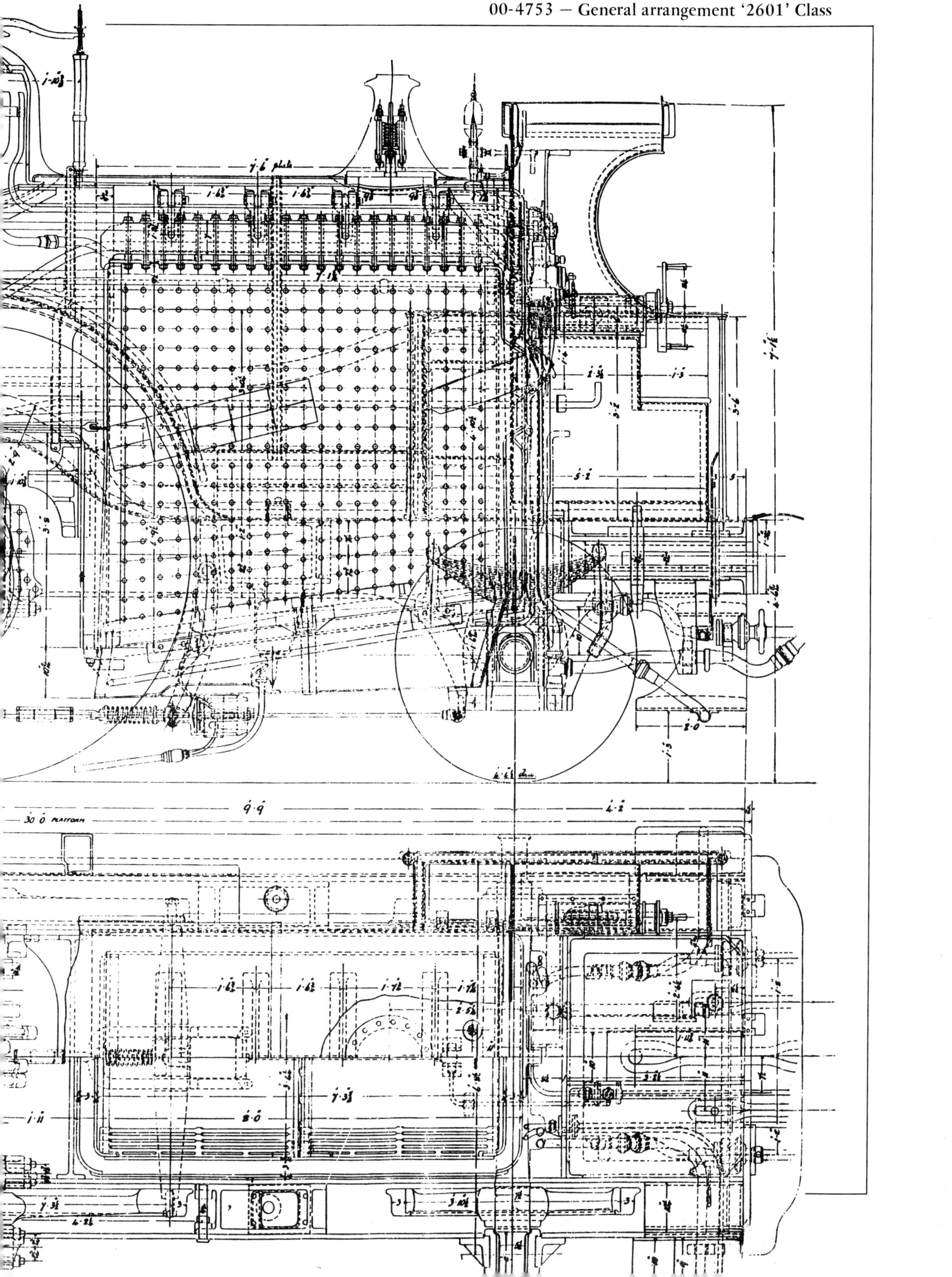

00-4753 — General arrangement '2601' Class

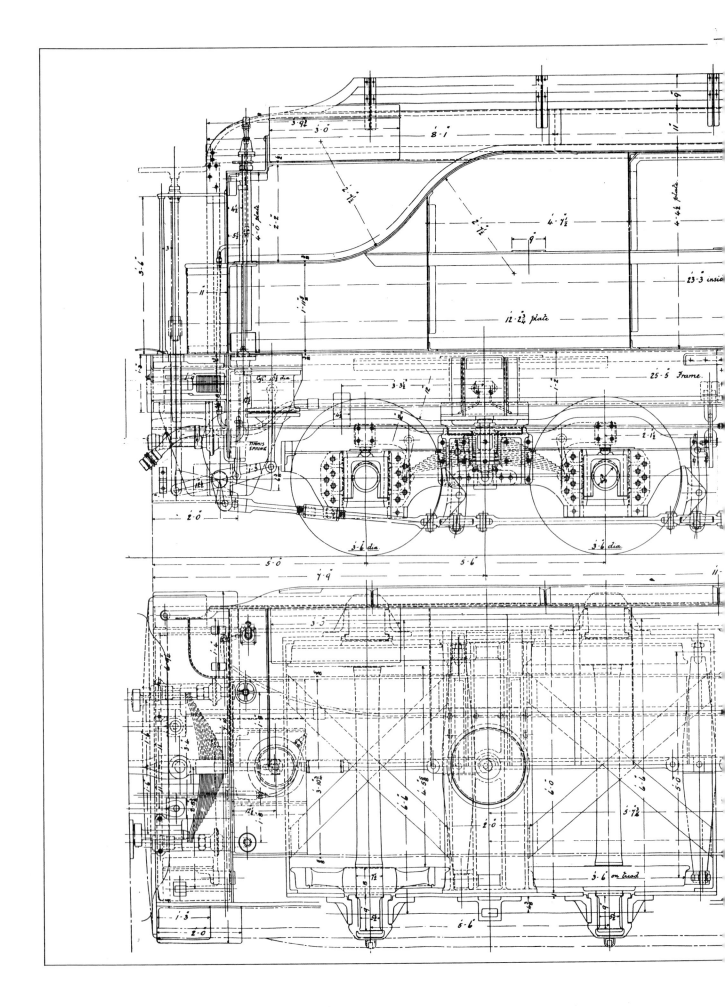

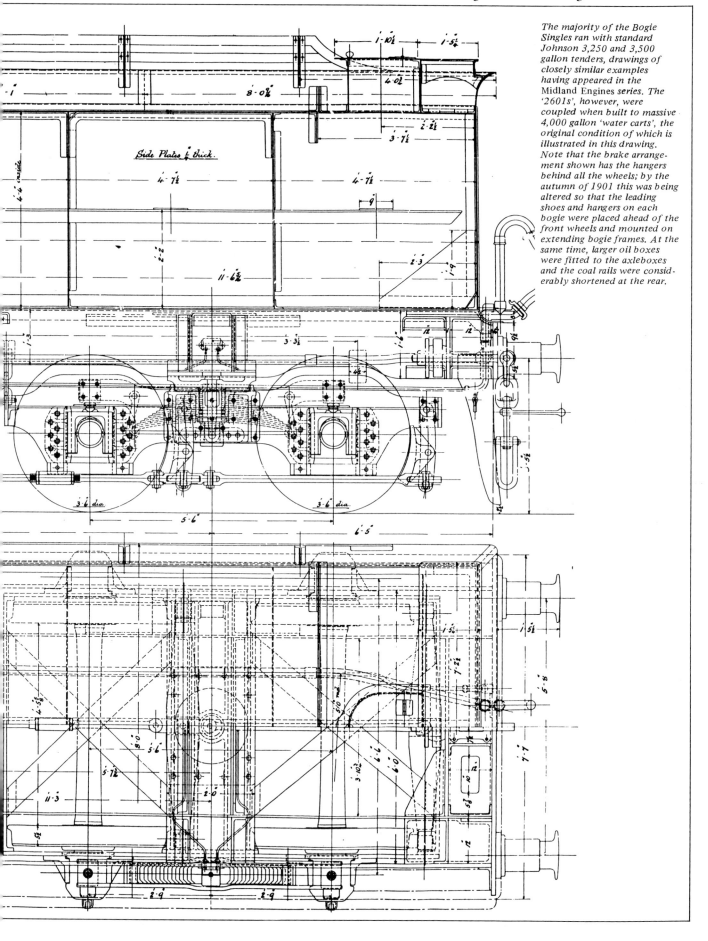

The majority of the Bogie Singles ran with standard Johnson 3,250 and 3,500 gallon tenders, drawings of closely similar examples having appeared in the Midland Engines series. The '2601s', however, were coupled when built to massive 4,000 gallon 'water carts', the original condition of which is illustrated in this drawing. Note that the brake arrangement shown has the hangers behind all the wheels; by the autumn of 1901 this was being altered so that the leading shoes and hangers on each bogie were placed ahead of the front wheels and mounted on extending bogie frames. At the same time, larger oil boxes were fitted to the axleboxes and the coal rails were considerably shortened at the rear.

Side Plates ½ thick.

The cab of a Johnson Bogie Single may have been visually appealing but, as this photograph shows, it provided hardly any real protection for the footplatemen and would have been quite cramped for the fireman to do his job. The locomotive shown was probably No. 1863.
COLLECTION R. J. ESSERY

EDITOR'S COMMENT
As someone who fired loco-motives with Johnson cabs, I am probably qualified to comment that running forward in dry weather, protection was reasonable, but running tender first in rain or snow, it was pretty awful. Fortunately, we often were able to use storm sheets but on occasions when they were not available I used to think whoever designed these engines never worked on them and I'd wish that we had a decent engine like a Class 3 or Class 4 0–6–0!

which eventually metamorphosed into the well-known Midland 20th-century shape begun with the Deeley Compounds. Let us not forget that Johnson had more to consider when designing a locomotive than whether the railway enthusiast would approve of its styling. With the '2601' Class he had to work with a bigger boiler and the requirement to provide a tender which could serve it in the absence of water troughs and I think that he and his draughtsmen did it brilliantly. Not only were they grace-ful machines, but they were purpose-ful and powerful looking without los-ing the elegance which characterised his nineteenth century designs. That Samuel Waite Johnson achieved visu-ally what he did with the last and biggest of the Bogie Singles is, to my mind, a measure of the man's supreme artistry. The first of the class, No. 2601, was named *Princess of Wales*, had flush-riveted smokebox wrapper and buffer beam like 1863 and 1867, and was sent to the Paris exhibition of 1900 where it won the Grand Prix, so it can't have been too ugly. End of author's message!

In summary, then, the leading particulars of the Bogie Singles as built were:

Class	'25'	'1853'	'1868'	'179'	'115'	'2601'
Boiler	D	D	D	D	E	F
Cylinders	18 x 26in	18½ x 26in	18½ x 26in	19 x 26in	19½ x 26in	19½ x 26in
Valves	Slide	Slide	Slide	Piston	Piston	Piston
Bogie wheels	3ft 6in	3ft 6in	3ft 6in	3ft 6in	3ft 9½in	3ft 10in
Driving wheels	7ft 4in	7ft 6in	7ft 6in	7ft 6in	7ft 9in	7ft 9½in
Carrying wheels	4ft 2½in	4ft 4in	4ft 4in	4ft 4in	4ft 4in	4ft 4½in
Weight in working order	43t 9c 3q	43t 9c 3q	44t 3c 0q	44t 4c 0q	47t 2c 1q	50t 3c 0q
Tender	3,250 gall	3,250 gall	3,250 gall	3,250 gall	3,500 gall	4,000 gall bogie

ALTERATIONS

The Bogie Singles escaped many of the alterations that befell other Johnson designs but there were still a number to be described. Ten of the '25' Class received 18½ in cylinders as below:

Engine (post-1907 nos. in brackets)	Date fitted 18½ in cylinders
25 (600)	Jan 1901
28 (603)	Dec 1895
29 (604)	Mar 1903
31 (606)	Jan 1903
37 (614)	Nov 1905
1857 (613)	May 1907
1858 (615)	Dec 1902
1859 (616)	Dec 1906
1861 (618)	Jun 1905
1862 (619)	May 1900

No. 618 then reverted to 18in cylin-ders in December 1907 and 600 followed suit in June 1910.

The '25' Class, '1853' Class and '1868' Class Nos. 1868–1872 that were built with sanding only ahead of the driving wheels proved unsatisfactory because if they had to set back with a train there was no sand to assist with traction. They were therefore altered sometime after 1892 to have sanding both sides of the driving wheels. Also from about 1892, the 3,250 gallon tenders coupled to slide valve engines were fitted with coal rails.

Carriage-warming apparatus was not fitted to the Bogie Singles as built until the '179' Class appeared in 1893 with the hot-water type. In the same year, Nos. 31, 170, 171, 1853, 1858, 1864, 1866 and 1870 were fitted with the system as they passed through the Works and some time later they were followed by Nos. 16,

This picture of No. 672 was taken at Derby when the locomotive was fitted with a parallel-sided chimney and dished smokebox door. Of particular interest are the allocation plates; the '3' on the smokebox door was for Saltley whilst the '10' on the cab front was for Leicester. COLLECTION R. J. ESSERY

17, 30, 97, 98, 129, 172, 173, 1860, 1861, 1867 and 1868. There may well have been more but records are sparse. In 1900, Nos. 177, 178, 1863, 1865 and 1872 were fitted with Laycock steam-heating apparatus but it was removed from 1863 and 1865 a year later for use on the M&GN. Neither the hot water nor the early steam systems were satisfactory, though, and it wasn't until 1903 that the type developed under Johnson and the Midland's Carriage & Wagon Superintendents, James Clayton and David Bain (Clayton retiring in 1902), was adopted for widespread use. Among the first engines converted in 1903 were Nos. 20–23, 117, 1863, 1864, 1866, 1867, 2601, 2603 and 2604. By 1908 all of the Bogie Singles except 75–77, 79, 88, and 126 had been equipped and although I can find no record that those engines were fitted, it would seem highly probable that they eventually were. At first, the steam pressure gauge for the Johnson & Bain system was about 6in diameter and positioned on the tender front plate adjacent to the coal hole but by about 1906 a smaller gauge was introduced and placed nearer to the tender side.

Around the turn of the twentieth century, tyre thickness on all except the '2601' Class was increased by ¼ in. Some engines, such as 31 and 176, had the Furness lubricators moved to the backs of the cylinders

in the same manner as the '2183' and '2203' Class 4-4-0s in about 1899. I don't know why this was done but suspect that it was to avoid passing the oil pipes through the waisted inner and outer smokebox wrappers.

In 1903 a centre lamp iron was fitted on the platform of all classes. The smokebox door lamp irons were removed from all except the '2601's, which, because of their higher-pitched boilers, had the top lamp irons removed but kept the smokebox door ones. From late 1904, the alarm whistles were removed and after 1906 some '179's, '115's, and '2601's were fitted with early-pattern sand ejectors.

The original arrangement of brakes on the '2601' Class bogie tenders was obviously unsatisfactory and by the autumn of 1901 they were being modified with the leading shoes and hangers on each bogie placed ahead of the front wheels, which involved extending the bogie frames at the front ends. The riding of the 'watercarts' was often noted as rough but I have been unable to discover whether the alteration of the brake arrangement was connected with it. At the same time, larger oil boxes were fitted to the axleboxes and the coal rails were shortened at the rear.

A fairly major alteration started by Deeley was the subject of O/3066 issued in December 1905, which stated that, 'When any engines having

boilers with drumhead tubeplates are in the shops for heavy repairs, the boilers must be fitted with new tubeplates of the ordinary type and new smokeboxes.' This was because the double skin of the drumhead smokeboxes was costly to maintain and the simpler, cheaper option of attaching the tubeplate to the barrel with an angle ring and flanging it into the smokebox wrapper served just as well. The new smokeboxes were flush riveted, about five inches larger in diameter than the drumhead type, and most were fitted from new with Deeley-pattern parallel-sided chimneys having large rims and capuchons, or wind guards as the Midland termed them. There were, however, a few instances of locomotives such as 611 and 675 carrying Johnson chimneys for a while on Deeley smokeboxes as well as Deeley smokebox doors appearing for a time on the Johnson smokeboxes of engines such as No. 94. The process of replacement does not seem to have taken very long, though, and by about 1908 all the Bogie Singles had Deeley smokeboxes and doors, most with parallel-sided chimneys, although a few unfortunates such as No. 683 received particularly revolting flowerpot versions for a while in 1907.

The first type of Deeley smokebox door fitted to the 4-2-2s was actually the second to be introduced and was flat with seven dogs spaced unevenly

No. 631 was built in 1892 as No. 122 of the '1868' Class and is seen here with the Deeley smokebox, door and parallel-sided capuchon chimney fitted prior to being renumbered in December 1907. The smokebox door was one of the flat type on a narrow seating ring with the dogs partly on the ring and partly on the front plate. As a purely subjective statement, I think that the changes did absolutely nothing for its appearance, although they were beneficial from an engineering point of view.

BRITISH RAILWAYS

round the periphery that were attached partly to a narrow seating ring and partly to the smokebox front plate. The one-piece Johnson handrail was retained and there was a small grab handle on the right-hand side. Problems were encountered with leakage from these doors and in 1910 a new dished type appeared with a wider seating ring, six dogs, separate straight handrail mounted below the top hinge, and no grab handle. The dogs were mounted wholly on the seating ring. Although the flat doors disappeared after a while, some engines, e.g., 600, 644, 663, 685 and 689, retained narrow seating rings with dished doors. After about 1920, replacement smokebox doors on all except the '2601's generally had wide seating rings, six dogs, and handrails mounted above the top hinge. There were still exceptions, though, such as 644 and 645, that retained narrow rings with seven dogs and low-mounted handrails with snap-riveted smokeboxes well after the Grouping and probably until withdrawal in April 1926 and August 1927 respectively. The '2601' Class appear to have retained the narrow seating rings with seven dogs and since their top lamp irons were positioned on the smokebox doors, none ever had the handrail above the top hinge.

Whilst Deeley's alterations sat well on Johnson's Edwardian passenger engine designs, the same can't be said of what he did to the Singles. In particular the chimney was, as far as I am concerned, a visual disaster. But then everyone has their prejudices.

The situation of straight Salter valve levers with D boilers but curved ones on E and F boilers only lasted until about 1907, after which there were examples such as 671, 673 and 678 carrying E boilers with straight levers and tall spring columns. After the First World War No. 600 had curved levers and short columns with its D boiler and 644 followed suit some time later, probably after the Grouping. Once again, there may well have been other examples of each category.

Some of the engines were reboilered at various times but always retained the class of boiler with which they had been built. None of the '2601' Class, however, was ever reboilered and all were withdrawn with the original units in place. One reason that the Singles escaped rebuilding in the way of the slim-boilered 4-4-0s was that larger boilers could not easily have been squeezed in between the large driving wheels. Deeley actually proposed rebuilding at least some of them as 4-4-0s with new rear frames, but although order numbers were allocated it never happened. The '2601' Class were to have had 7ft 0in driving wheels whilst eight '25' Class and two '1853' Class engines would have had 6ft 6in ones and cylinders enlarged to 18½ in, all with 9ft 6in wheelbases and G8 Belpaire boilers pressed to 200 psi. Original tenders would have been retained. Apart from some sketches and a frame drawing, little seems to have been done about the proposal.

The other major alteration was the rebuilding of the '2601' Class bogie tenders into 3,500 gallon 6-wheelers after water troughs were brought into use on the main lines. O/3698 was issued on 15th March 1910 for rebuilding them and at first it was intended that they should go to 'Belpaire' 4-4-0s with the Bogie Singles receiving 3,250 gallon examples but in the event they were returned to Nos. 685–694. The original idea was to keep the forward plates of the tank sides unaltered and to reduce the rear part by 3ft 6½ in, which would have displaced the vertical butt strips, or 'beading' well to the rear of the tanks. In the event, the two side plates were shortened by an equal amount and the butt strips were central. When altered, the 'water carts' ended up very similar to the standard Deeley 3,500 gallon design but with higher side sheets to the coal spaces and turned-under frames below the platforms, as did the rebuilt Compound bogie tenders. Sadly for these grand locomotives, what the Deeley alterations did for them at the front end, the rebuilt tenders complemented at the rear. During the First World War, at least Nos. 687 and 691 were fitted with crude tender cabs with tarpaulins stretched between the locomotive and tender cab roofs.

The first Bogie Single to be built, No. 25/600, was selected in January 1917 for fitting with motor train gear for use with the General Superintendent's saloon, which was ex-steam railmotor No. 2234. The locomotive received vacuum control regulator and whistle equipment from 0-4-4 tank engine No. 1252 to O/5001 in March the same year, the order also covering overhaul of the driving apparatus fitted to the carriage. In addition, the locomotive was fitted with a Deeley-style upper cab closely similar to those fitted to H-boilered goods engines whilst retaining its original cab sides, or handrail plates as the Midland referred to them.[11] In 1923 a drawing was prepared for fitting coal watering apparatus to 600's tender so that dust could be damped down but I can't state whether it was actually installed.

After the Grouping, ten of the '115' Class, Nos. 670–673, 676–679, 682 and 683, had their original tenders replaced with 2,950 gallon ones that they retained until withdrawal. It is one of these tenders that is coupled to the preserved No. 673 at the NRM today.

THE ENGINES IN SERVICE

At least some of the Singles became known as 'Spinners', although I have heard and read at least two explanations for the derivation of the name and two versions of which engines were so christened. The most common story (including from the Editor – so it must be right!) is that the '115' Class were the first to be called 'Spinners' but that the term later came to include all the 4-2-2s. Apparently it was applied to them either because they had a noted tendency to slip, or 'spin', on starting, or because of the phenomenon observed by Hamilton Ellis when he wrote, 'It was the effect of the big driving wheels turning without visible connecting rods – they swept along in quite a different way.' In other words, they seemed to 'spin' along the track. Take your pick.

The vast majority of the work carried out by the 4-2-2s when they entered service was on the Derby and Nottingham–London, Derby–Bristol,

The final nail in the appearance of some '2601's was visited on them during the First World War when they had crude tender cabs fitted for blackout purposes, as shown in this picture of No. 691. The engine was built as No. 2607, renumbered 20 upon entering service, and lasted until 1920. It is sad to see the state to which these superb engines were brought in the final years of their existence when compared with the photographs of 2601 and 21 in their heyday.
COLLECTION R. J. ESSERY

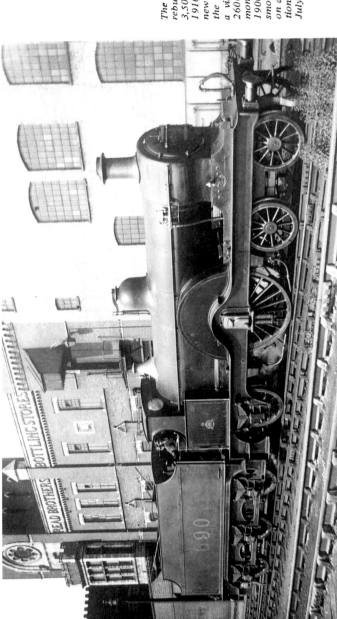

The '2601' Class bogie tenders were rebuilt into almost standard Deeley 3,500 gallon 6-wheelers from March 1910. Unfortunately, nothing about the new tenders lined up with anything on the locomotives and the ensemble was a visual disaster. No. 690 was built as 2606 but renumbered 19 a couple of months after entering service in July 1900. It is seen here with a Deeley smokebox and fittings, the dished door on a narrow seating ring, in which condition it remained until withdrawal in July 1922.
COLLECTION
R. J. ESSERY

Liverpool–Chinley and CLC passenger trains. Nottingham and Kentish Town were the first recipients, followed by Bristol, Liverpool Brunswick, Leicester, Saltley, Bedford and Derby. Up to about 1907 or 1908, this pattern didn't change apart from some engines moving between the sheds already mentioned, then, as they were replaced on the more important turns by the newer 4–4–0s, some were sent to Gloucester, Kettering and Peterborough.

The First World War had its effects on the whole British railway system, but there can't have been a much more bizarre one than the despatch of Bogie Singles to Toton for use on the Brent mineral trains. If ever a locomotive type was unsuited to slow goods work it was the Johnson 4–2–2 but needs must, there was a dire shortage of goods engines, and several Singles were under-utilised at their home depots. Starting in August 1915, at least Nos. 601, 605, 630–633, 646–650, 658 and 681–684 were so employed whilst increasing numbers of others were stored out of use as passenger services were withdrawn. Even though they were never again used intensively as a class on express passenger work, the 4–2–2s could still be seen on ordinary passenger trains on the routes for which they had been built as well as 606, 617, 638, 643, 645, 667, 669, 676 and 680 working around Leeds and Normanton in 1920 and 1921.

Withdrawal began in July 1919 with Nos. 601 and 686, although these engines had been out of use for at least three and two years respectively and neither actually had a boiler! In September 1920 No. 609 went, then starting in the autumn of 1921 there was a massive cull of out-of-use engines and by the summer of 1922 all the '1853' and '2601' Classes and all but two of the '25' Class had gone. The LMS inherited 43 of them: Nos. 600 and 614 of the '25' Class; Nos. 627, 628, 632, 633, 635, 638–641, 643–645, 649, 651, 652, 654, 655, 657 and 659 of the '1868' Class; all the '179' Class; and all but Nos. 675, 681 and 684 of the '115' Class. No further withdrawals took place until March

1925 but from then on they came thick and fast as engines fell due for repair, until by the end of 1927 only three were left. Nos. 673 and 679 were withdrawn from Saltley in March 1928 and the last survivor, quite fittingly I suppose, was the first of its kind, number 25/600, which lasted until the following autumn at Nottingham, having been relieved of its inspection saloon duties in late 1927. As already stated, 673 was saved from the torch and can now be admired in the National Railway Museum.

The later singles were not long-lived engines by Midland standards, although some of the earlier ones lasted over thirty years. It has to be remembered, however, that they weren't rebuilt. Some notably aged Midland locomotives had in fact undergone lots of rebuilding, and as regards original fabric were probably akin to the genuine medieval axe which has only had two new heads and three new handles.

Although they seem to have been well liked, and despite steam sanding, the 4–2–2s needed careful handling when starting or pulling hard. Many years after the last one had been withdrawn, Sir Henry Fowler said that the crank axles of the Bogie Singles had been a constant source of trouble, due mainly to cracks developing, and that none of them lasted longer than eight years. Whether this tendency to crack was thought to be due to the strains set up by slips, greater than normal flange pressure because of the large diameter of the wheels, a combination of the two or some other reason, he didn't indicate.

LIVERY

Livery of the Bogie Singles was a complex matter. They were held in great esteem by many people and, as a consequence, seem to have attracted lots of attention from the painters. Robert Weatherburn was recorded by P. C. Dewhurst as having five favourite locomotives, which were Nos. 1856, 1860, 1870, 1871 and 117. All received not only the full Weatherburn treatment, or 'London style', but had extra embellishment. The first three mentioned even had the vacuum hose stand pipes special-

ly lined. Engines allocated to Kentish Town would almost certainly have had the extra ornate livery, possibly including such things as polished top edges of main frames and fronts of guard irons. Dewhurst noted that in the case of No. 2601, 'The spring pin heads were polished'. Kentish Town's stud of Bogie Singles in 1901 comprised Nos. 75–77, 116, 117, 130, 131, 1853, 1854, 1856–1860, 1870–1872 and 2601–2604, but there had been others stationed there which would probably still show the ornate painting style for some time after. Other depots such as Bristol also had their special painting styles in the *fin de siècle* years, which Dewhurst maintained was a result of Johnson's encouragement of his men to take a pride in their work. Thus it would be a monumental task to describe the livery of every Johnson Single from cradle to grave and I'm not going to try. What I will attempt is a broad brush (no pun intended) treatment and leave it largely to photographic evidence. I am indebted to Jack Braithwaite for much of the above information and some of what follows.

If there was such a thing as a 'standard' paint scheme for the Singles when they were built it would probably have been as follows: Frames, splashers, boiler clothing, cab sides and fronts, wheels, sandboxes, guard irons, brake hangers and footstep supports were red, whilst platforms, splasher tops, footsteps, cab roofs, smokeboxes, chimneys and tyres were black. Lining was applied to the edges of frames, footstep supports, sandboxes, guard irons (inside and out), brake hangers, axleboxes, the top leaves of springs, splashers, tyres and wheel centres. The bases of dome covers, cab side lower and upper panels, spectacle plates and boiler clothing bands were also lined, but the spectacles and angle between boiler clothing and cab front weren't. Buffer planks, buffer housings and the insides of frames were vermilion with buffer planks and housings lined out. Spectacle frames, safety valve covers, whistles, Salter valve columns, splasher beading and axlebox covers on the helical spring engines were polished brass. Handrails and buffers were polished

No. 665, built as 75 in April 1896, was photographed at Kentish Town in May 1924 with its ownership indicated by the small gold 'L M S' characters on the cab sides rather than the more usual 'button' crest. It had a later-pattern Deeley smokebox door with handrail above the top hinge and mounted on a wide seating ring and the builders' plates were still on the front framing.   COLLECTION R. J. ESSERY

Taken at Farnley Junction on 30th June 1925, this photograph shows No. 679, ex-125 of the '115' Class, prepared for the celebrations surrounding the centenary of the Stockton and Darlington Railway. Snap-head rivets had been used on the splasher tops and cab sides, and the builders' plates had been moved to the splasher sides. To be more accurate, the old Midland builders' plates had been replaced with new ones bearing the legend 'LMS BUILT 1899 DERBY'. This was also the case with other engines on which the plates were moved to the splasher sides.   REAL PHOTOGRAPHS

steel. The diamond crest was carried on the splasher sides, gold shaded sans serif 'M R' on the buffer planks, and brass numbers were mounted on the cab sides. Inside the cab was grained oak finish above waist level and lined red below. Tender frames, tank sides and rears, front bulkheads, tool boxes, springs, axleboxes, guard irons, brake hangers and wheels were red, and platforms, tank tops, coal rails, footsteps and tyres black. Frames, spring buckles, axleboxes, brake hangers, guard irons, bulkheads and tool boxes were edge lined. Sometimes the beading at the tops and bottoms of the tank sides and rears were painted black and edged yellow on the upper edges. The beading on the flare was also painted black and sometimes had a yellow line on the lower edge. Tank sides and rears had lined panels inset from the beading. Tyres were lined as the locomotives. Buffer planks and housings were lined vermilion and the insides of frames were also vermilion. After 1892 gold, shaded serif 'M R' appeared on the tank sides, one letter being placed in the centre of each panel. Prior to 1898 sans serif 'M R' would also have been seen on the tender buffer planks, but after this time it was moved onto the rear of the tanks. There were some instances, however, of serif letters being applied to the buffer planks.

Even apart from the 'special' treatment applied to some engines, though, there were variations on this 'basic' livery. Such additions as lining on the springs could be seen, and the only way to be sure of an individual engine's livery is to study photographs.

The only other thing I will go into concerning Johnson era livery is the 'London style' as described by P. C. Dewhurst. The red of the Kentish Town engines, he averred, was a darker and richer shade than that used elsewhere. The lining, instead of being straw colour, was white, or nearly so, and was wider than usual. Extra lining was applied to the boiler clothing around the base of the safety valve cover, spectacle frames, on the axle ends, spring buckle anchorages of the bogie, penultimate top

and bottom leaves of trailing and tender springs, and spring buckles. On some engines the crests were also outlined, with a double line below and to the right. Wheel spokes had stripes with vees at the rim and boss, and vees were also painted on the tops of trailing wheel and tender axlebox spring hangers. The lining on trailing and tender axleboxes was extended to the angled faces as well as the outer faces. Splasher tops had lined red panels on the front portions. Occasionally extra lining panels were added to the cab sides inside the normal edge lining. Some engines, known as 'yellow bellies', had the underside of the boiler clothing forward of the splashers painted cream to reflect light onto the polished motion. Others, such as No. 1856, had this area painted white. This was not a 'standard' Kentish Town livery because there were variations and additions, some of them really too florid, but it was fairly common. As already stated, there were other 'special' liveries applied to the Singles, but it would take far too long in an article such as this to describe every variation, even if I could get close to a satisfactory coverage.

Once Deeley took over at Derby, the Singles were treated as any other class. From about 1905 onwards the livery was simplified. One of the first things to change was that the lining on tenders was moved to the beading and the inset lining panels were omitted. Initially, the centre beading was lined and 'M R' still appeared on the tank sides. Further simplification resulted in the boiler clothing bands being unlined except for the rear of the one next to the smokebox and front of the angle between firebox clothing and spectacle plate. Adornments round the bases of domes were omitted and the running numbers were moved to the tender sides where they appeared in 18in gold shaded black transfers. Cast number plates were fixed onto Deeley smokebox doors. Initially the diamond crest was retained, although moved to the cab sides, but after about 1906 the Company coat-of-arms was used instead. Springs, axleboxes, guard irons, frames above the

platforms, beading and wheels were painted black, the latter having a yellow line around the rim. Lining of the centre beading on tender sides was removed and there were no initials to show ownership on tender buffer planks or tank rears. The embellishments used at Kentish Town and other depots were discontinued and there was much more uniformity. These changes did not, however, happen overnight, and anomalies could be seen for some time. Once again, the only way to be sure of an individual locomotive's painting details during the transition phase between Johnson and Deeley is to study photographs of it.

Because they didn't last beyond the 1928 livery change, the Johnson Singles never wore the LMS funereal black which would probably have been their lot had they survived longer. The only changes to the Midland livery were removal of the buffer plank initials and replacement of the cab side arms either by the 'button' crest or, in the case of at least No. 665, small 'L M S' gold shaded black transfers. Even these changes didn't happen overnight, and it is probable that many of the Singles were withdrawn still displaying Midland ownership. The three engines which lasted into 1928 ended their days still in red livery.

POSTSCRIPT
The Bogie Singles weren't particularly advanced machines technologically, although they did pioneer the use of piston valves and cast steel wheels on the Midland, nor was their performance in service exceptional. They were, however, adequate for the work allocated to them, surprisingly so in some instances given the potential limitations of their wheel arrangement, and apart from trouble with crank axles seem to have been fairly reliable. The '2601' Class probably represented the practical size limit for 4–2–2s and it may be significant that they were the shortest lived. What can definitely be stated is that they were beautiful machines and the world would have been the poorer without them. As usual, I have tried to get it right, but if anyone out

No. when built	Date built	Renumbered	Date	Withdrawn
25	Jun 1887	600	Sep 1907	Jul 1928
26	Jul 1887	601	Aug 1907	Jul 1919
27	Jul 1887	602	Dec 1907	Jan 1922
28	Aug 1887	603	Nov 1907	Jan 1922
29	Aug 1887	604	Jul 1907	Jan 1922
30	Dec 1888	605	Sep 1907	Oct 1921
31	Dec 1888	606	Nov 1907	Jan 1922
32	Dec 1888	607	Aug 1907	Jan 1922
1853	Feb 1889	608	Jun 1907	Nov 1921
34	Mar 1889	609	Aug 1907	Sep 1920
1854	Jun 1889	610	Jun 1907	Jan 1922
1855	Jul 1889	611	Oct 1907	Feb 1922
1856	Aug 1889	612	Nov 1907	Nov 1921
1857	Aug 1889	613	Sep 1907	Feb 1922
37	Aug 1889	614	Sep 1907	Sep 1925
1858	Sep 1889	615	Sep 1907	Mar 1922
1859	Oct 1889	616	Dec 1907	Feb 1922
1860	Oct 1889	617	Sep 1907	Nov 1921
1861	Oct 1889	618	Jul 1907	Nov 1921
1862	Jan 1890	619	Jul 1907	Nov 1921
1863	Nov 1889	620	Jul 1907	Feb 1922
1864	Nov 1889	621	Jul 1907	Nov 1921
1865	Dec 1889	622	Jul 1907	Nov 1921
1866	Jan 1890	623	Oct 1907	Nov 1921
1867	Feb 1890	624	Oct 1907	Feb 1922
1868	Jan 1891	625	Oct 1907	Feb 1922
1869	Jan 1891	626	Jul 1907	Mar 1922
1870	Feb 1891	627	May 1907	Apr 1925
1871	Feb 1891	628	Jul 1907	Apr 1926
1872	Feb 1891	629	Jul 1907	Nov 1921
8	May 1892	630	Oct 1907	Oct 1921
122	May 1892	631	Dec 1907	Oct 1921
20	May 1892	132	Jul 1900	Oct 1926
		632	Dec 1907	
145	May 1892	633	Nov 1907	Jun 1927
24	Jun 1892	634	Aug 1907	Jan 1922
33	Jun 1892	635	Nov 1907	Mar 1925
35	Jul 1892	636	Oct 1907	Nov 1921
36	Jul 1892	637	Jun 1907	Nov 1921
38	Jul 1892	638	Sep 1907	Nov 1927
39	Jul 1892	639	Oct 1907	Apr 1925
4	Sep 1892	640	Aug 1907	Apr 1927
16	Sep 1892	641	Oct 1907	Aug 1927
17	Oct 1892	642	Oct 1907	Nov 1921
94	Oct 1892	643	Apr 1907	Mar 1925
97	Oct 1892	644	Sep 1907	Apr 1926
98	Nov 1892	645	Jun 1907	Aug 1927
99	Nov 1892	646	Oct 1907	Oct 1921
100	Nov 1892	647	Dec 1907	Nov 1921
129	Dec 1892	648	Dec 1907	Nov 1921
133	Dec 1892	649	Jun 1907	Nov 1927
149	Feb 1893	650	Sep 1907	Oct 1921
170	Feb 1893	651	Oct 1907	Jun 1926
171	Feb 1893	652	Aug 1907	Jun 1925
172	Feb 1893	653	Dec 1907	Nov 1921
173	Mar 1893	654	Jul 1907	Apr 1925
174	Mar 1893	655	Jul 1907	Aug 1925
175	Apr 1893	656	Nov 1907	Nov 1921
176	Apr 1893	657	Oct 1907	Mar 1925
177	May 1893	658	Aug 1907	Nov 1921
178	May 1893	659	Aug 1907	Apr 1925
179	Sep 1893	660	Aug 1907	Jan 1926
180	Oct 1893	661	Oct 1907	Dec 1926
181	Nov 1893	662	Dec 1907	Sep 1926
182	Dec 1893	663	Apr 1907	Apr 1926
183	Dec 1893	664	Nov 1907	Jun 1926
75	Apr 1896	665	Sep 1907	Jan 1926
76	May 1896	666	Jun 1907	Apr 1925
77	Jun 1896	667	Sep 1907	Mar 1925
79	Jun 1896	668	Dec 1907	Apr 1925
88	Jun 1896	669	Aug 1907	Apr 1927
115	Nov 1896	670	July 1907	Jan 1926

there has more or better information please let me know.

It is one of these engines, built as No. 118, that has fortunately been preserved in its post-1907 state as No. 673. Even though it lacks a flush smokebox fronted by a subtly contoured door and surmounted by a Johnson chimney, as well as being coupled to a 2,950 gallon tender, it is still, in both my opinion and that of many others, the most beautiful of all preserved locomotives.

NOTES IN TEXT

1. I am aware that some of the engines were built in 1900 and that there is a school of thought which regards that year as the opening of the 20th century. As there was no year zero, however, I subscribe to the argument that 1900 years after the birth of Christ was the year 1900 and the first year of the 20th century was therefore 1901. Well, you have to take a stand on some issues.

2. One single driver engine, No. 4, was produced at Derby Works in 1869 but it was a rebuild of an 1861 locomotive and not a new one.

3. Goods engines tended to haul heavier loads and so required a higher tractive effort to get their trains under way. One way of achieving this with the same steam pressure and cylinder size was to reduce the size of the driving wheels. To absorb such increased tractive effort without slipping, the power was transmitted to two or more axles via coupling rods; hence, goods engines sometimes differed from contemporary express passenger engines simply by having two or more axles of smaller, coupled wheels.

4. One problem associated with steel tyres, particularly in frosty weather, was that of them suddenly breaking in several places simultaneously rather than at one point as would normally be the case with stress fractures. Ahrons suggested that the problem may have had three causes: a relatively high sulphur content in the steel that made the tyres more brittle at low temperatures; too much work done on the tyres at critical temperatures during manufacture; and variable shrinkage allowed when fitting the tyres, placing them under undue stress. If such a relatively brittle, stressed tyre was subjected to a very cold and, therefore unyielding, track, it could well shatter without warning, as was sometimes seen. Eventually these factors were eliminated and, in any event, the advantages of steel tyres vastly outweighed the drawback.

5. I have seen it stated that the Westinghouse Company raised objections to what it saw as an abuse of its equipment following the first trials of Holt's air sanding system but haven't been able to find any primary evidence of it.

6. At that time, the letter classification for boilers was not in general use. Although

there were references to 'P' and 'C' class boilers in Midland documents of the 1880s, they referred to those on passenger engines and Class 'C' locomotives. The next letter designation seems to have been applied to the B boiler in 1891 when it was used to refer to the type of boiler fitted to outside contractor-built 'Class B' Johnson 0-6-0s. It wasn't until the late 1890s, though, that the now familiar Midland boiler classifications came into general use.

7. The figure I have quoted comes from the Derby drawing schedules for the '25' and '1853' Classes. The 1903 Engine Diagram, however, gives the chimney height as 3ft 4in.

8. As far as the Midland Locomotive department was concerned, all engines had inside and outside frames. Even the platform angles, or what are sometimes called valances, on such as the 4-4-0s, Class 3 and 4 goods engines and 0-4-4 tanks were referred to as outside frames.

9. It still took a Parliamentary Act of 1900 and Board of Trade 1904 regulation before the Midland was finally forced to do away with rear toolboxes on all its tenders, though.

10. This was actually in contravention of the Civil Engineers clearance for 17½ tons maximum axle loading and from July 1897 the springing was adjusted to reduce the weight on the driving wheels to 18 tons. Two months later, clearance was given for the full 18½ tons between Derby and Nottingham, Bristol and London.

11. It is possible that some of the materials used in 600's upper cab came from an H-boilered 0-6-0 being rebuilt with a Belpaire boiler.

ALLOCATIONS

Allocations when new. This is taken from a list compiled by Walter Laidlaw.

District	Locomotives allocated when new
Bedford	4, 16, 24,
Bristol	34, 37, 33, 35–39, 88, 94, 97, 98, 128, 181–183
Derby	75, 127, 145, 149, 180, 2606–2610
Kentish Town	25–27, 76, 77, 116, 117, 130, 131, 1853–1862, 1870, 2601, 2603, 2604
Leicester	118, 170–178, 1871, 1872
Liverpool	8, 1863–1866
Nottingham	20, 28–32, 79, 115, 120– 125, 2602, 2605
Saltley	99, 100, 122, 126, 129, 133

31st March 1892. This is taken from a list compiled by E. L. Ahrons.

District	Locomotives allocated
Bedford	34, 37
Kentish Town	25–29, 1853–1862
Leicester	1871, 1872
Liverpool	1863–1866
Nottingham	30–32, 1867–1870

31st May 1908. This is taken from a list compiled by F. H. Clarke.

District	Locomotives allocated
Bedford	4, 16, 17, 24, 179, 1859, 1861, 1867–1869
Bristol	32–39, 88, 94, 97–100, 180–183
Derby	127–131, 145, 149
Kentish Town	19–23, 1853, 1854, 1856, 1858, 1860, 2601–2604
Kettering	1855, 1857
Leicester	1870–1872, 170–178, 116–119
Liverpool	1862–1866
Nottingham	25–31, 79, 115, 120, 123–125, 2605
Saltley	75–77, 121, 122, 126, 132, 133

30th April 1914. This is taken from an official Midland Railway list.

District	Locomotives allocated
Bedford	616–618, 624–626, 634, 640–642, 660
Bristol	607, 614, 609, 635–639, 643–645, 669, 661–664
Derby	633, 646–648, 650, 681–684
Gloucester	604, 606, 668
Kentish Town	608, 610–613, 615, 619–63, 685–688, 690–694
Kettering	603
Leicester	627–629, 651–659, 671–674
Liverpool	619, 620–623
Nottingham	601, 605, 670, 675, 677–679, 689
Peterborough	600, 602
Saltley	631, 632, 649, 665–667, 676, 680

30th November 1920. This is taken from a General Superintendent's office list.

District	Locomotives allocated
Bedford	618, 624–626, 634, 641, 660
Bristol	607, 614, 635, 636, 639, 648, 661, 662, 664, 665, 670
Derby	600, 644
Gloucester	604, 668
Kentish Town	608, 610, 611, 613, 615, 685–692
Kettering	627, 666, 693, 694
Leeds	617, 638, 643, 645, 667, 669, 680
Leicester	628, 629, 651, 652, 653 - 657, 659, 671, 673, 674
Liverpool	616, 620, 623
Normanton	606, 676
Nottingham	675, 677–679
Peterborough	602 619, 621, 622, 637, 663
Toton	605, 630–633, 646, 647, 649, 650, 658, 681, 682, 684
Wellingborough	603, 640, 642, 672

No. when built	Date built	Renumbered	Date	Withdrawn
116	Dec 1896	671	Sep 1907	Dec 1926
117	Feb 1897	672	May 1907	Sep 1926
118	Mar 1897	673	Jul 1907	Apr 1928
119	Mar 1897	674	Jun 1907	Mar 1925
120	Jan 1899	675	Jul 1907	Nov 1921
121	Jan 1899	676	Jul 1907	Aug 1925
123	Jan 1899	677	Jul 1907	Aug 1926
124	Feb 1899	678	Jul 1907	Aug 1926
125	Feb 1899	679	Oct 1907	Mar 1928
126	Mar 1899	680	Jun 1907	Sep 1926
127	Mar 1899	681	Jun 1907	Jan 1922
128	Apr 1899	682	May 1907	Dec 1926
130	Apr 1899	683	May 1907	Apr 1926
131	Apr 1899	684	May 1907	Oct 1921
2601	Dec 1899	685	May 1907	Nov 1921
2602	Jan 1900	686	Oct 1907	Jul 1919
2603	Jan 1900	687	Sep 1907	Mar 1922
2604	Feb 1900	688	Nov 1907	Mar 1922
2605	Mar 1900	689	Apr 1907	Mar 1922
2606	May 1900	19	Jul 1900	Jul 1922
		690	Dec 1907	
2607	May 1900	20	Jul 1900	Mar 1922
		691	Nov 1907	
2608	Jun 1900	21	Jul 1900	Nov 1921
		692	Dec 1907	
2609	Jun 1900	22	Jul 1900	Nov 1921
		693	Sep 1907	
2610	Jun 1900	23	Jul 1900	Nov 1921
		694	Oct 1907	

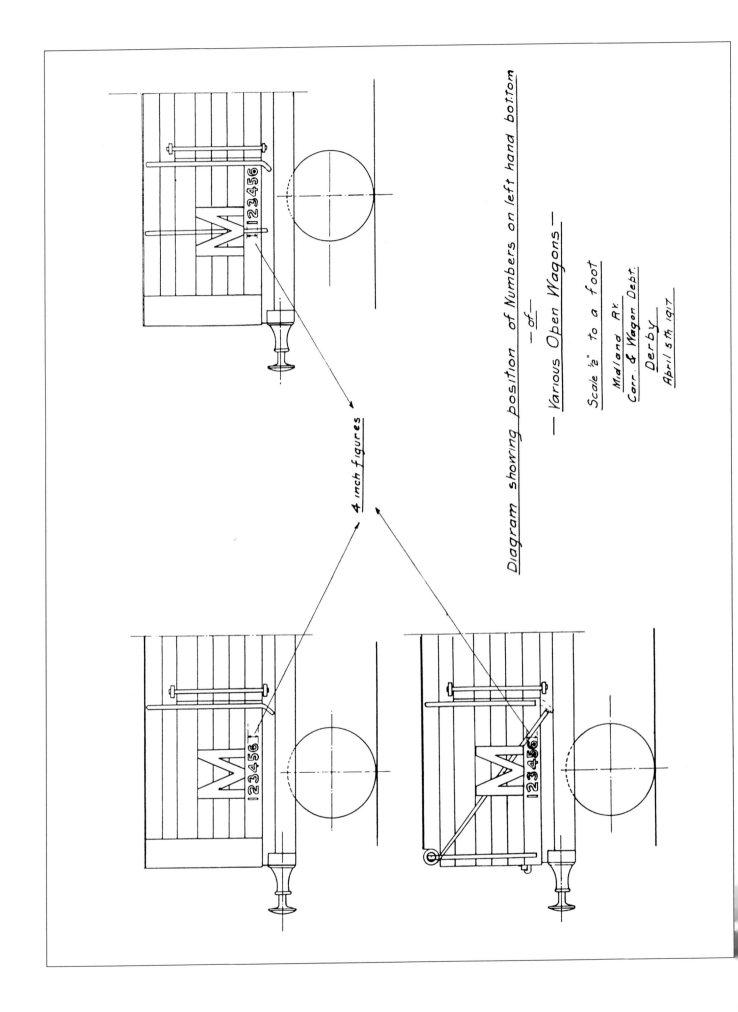

Diagram showing position of Numbers on left hand bottom
— of —
— Various Open Wagons —

Scale ½" to a foot

Midland Ry.
Carr. & Wagon Dept.
Derby
April 5th 1917

4 inch figures

M 123456

MIDLAND RAILWAY WAGON LETTERING

Notes by BOB ESSERY

This undated picture of No. 55160 was probably taken at about the same time as 69403 overleaf and was for use in a training document illustrating the correct and incorrect methods of loading. This example was to show the method of roping bales of hay before the load was covered by a wagon sheet. The wagon is an example of D299, the most numerous of all Midland wagon types. COLLECTION R. J. ESSERY

Chapter Two of *Midland Wagons Vol. 1*, published in 1980 by OPC, was entitled 'Livery – An Outline of Practice'. This book was my first solo effort. Following the launch of *Midland Record* in 1994, we were able to publish additional information, including a supplement devoted to the Company's freight rolling stock - *Midland Record Supplement No. 2: Midland Railway Wagons* (1998. Wild Swan Publications). Notwithstanding all that was written since 1980, neither I nor any 'wagon enthusiast' that I know had drawn attention to a variation in respect of the painting of numbers on certain open wagons during the Midland Railway period. This short article is an attempt to add a little more to the story.

Recently I obtained this drawing, which is dated 5th April 1917. It is self-explanatory and shows how the wagon number was to be painted on the left-hand bottom plank, or board, as it was described on the drawing. This instruc-

tion was sent to the works; there is a pencil note on the drawing, '6 off today', at a time when the Great War was raging, so the question arises, why was the change made? The only explanation I have was that when the wagon side doors were lowered, the cast-iron numberplate was obscured and the wagon number could not easily be seen. Maybe during peacetime this did not matter but during the war, with less staff available, it was felt that by repositioning the wagon number, the work of recording wagon stock at goods stations would be made easier. That is the only theory I can offer. It will be interesting to see what other suggestions readers come up with. When we begin to revise and prepare a new edition of *LMS Wagons*, it will be necessary to examine with care the information available about painting styles inherited from the constituent companies and then adopted by the LMS.

Although an illustration of this wagon with the side door open appears in Midland Wagons *Vol. 1, I felt that the inclusion of this picture of No. 69403 could be used to show an example of D607 12-ton coal wagon. This was a newly painted vehicle that was photographed on 28th June 1918, displaying the wagon number as per the new instruction.*
COLLECTION
R. J. ESSERY

In Midland Record *No. 14 we published an article about D351 8-ton high-sided wagons and included a picture of wagon No. 112709. Here we show the end view of the same wagon that illustrates the new practice of placing the wagon number below the 'M', although on the opposite side of the vehicle the 'M' and wagon number would be at the fixed end of the wagon. The final picture in this article also showed the LMS practice of placing the tare weight below the wagon number, but this was a later variation.*
COLLECTION R. J. ESSERY

I have included this picture of a D299 No. 124124 to show how the side door, when in the open position, obscured the wagon number-plate and why it was sensible to paint the wagon number at the end of the bottom plank so that it was always visible. I assume this picture was taken in order to show the correct method of loading sacks in an open goods wagon prior to sheeting over to protect the contents from the weather.
COLLECTION
R. J. ESSERY

This train of new 'LMS' wagons, built to Midland Railway drawing 5612 and lettered 'LMS' but fitted with Midland Railway cast-iron number plates, was taken on 12th March 1923. It has been included to show that new construction from Derby followed Midland practice and it would be interesting to know what painting styles the other LMS wagon works followed during 1923. In many respects it can be considered as being transitional and not dissimilar to what happened in 1948 when evidence of the old and new order could be seen on the same vehicle at the same time.
COLLECTION R. J. ESSERY

 MIDLAND TERRITORY

This picture is described in the Midland Railway Photograph Register as 'Girder in position' and shows the new girder with the supporting timbers below.
NATIONAL RAILWAY MUSEUM (DY4189)

BROMHAM VIADUCT

Notes by BOB ESSERY

This picture was taken looking north through the girders towards Oakley Junction with the Down Home signals clearly visible in the distance.
NATIONAL RAILWAY MUSEUM (DY4186)

Bromham Viaduct was between Oakley Junction and Bedford on the Leicester and Hitchin line. The two pictures were part of a series; 4184/5 were of the old viaduct and 4186-4194 illustrated the new one. They were taken to show work on the replacement viaduct over the River Ouse, which, as can be seen from the accompanying Distance Diagram, ran below the railway seven times between Sharnbrook and Bedford for a length of just over 7½ miles. Between Bedford North and Oakley Junction the passenger lines were closed from 10th May 1891 to allow rebuilding of the new viaduct until four-track working was restored on completion of the work on 14th February 1892. According to John Gough's *Chronology*, a temporary signal box was opened on 10th May 1891 and it was closed on 14th February 1892. This would be normal practice for work of this nature but he also records that a second signal box was opened on 20th May 1902, which remained open until 19th July 1967.

Unfortunately, I do not have any pictures of the old viaduct, so I would be particularly interested if any reader can supply a print of it to complete the story.

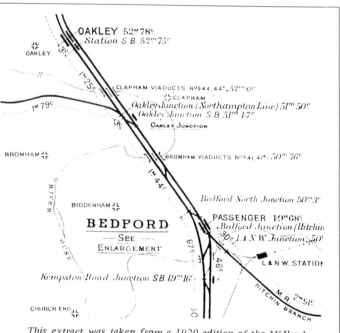

This extract was taken from a 1920 edition of the Midland Railway Distance Diagram and shows the location of Bromham Viaduct and the River Ouse. Although the 1902 signal box is not shown on the diagram, it does appear on an enlargement of Bedford, which does not show the viaduct. The 1902 Bromham signal box was 50 miles 57 chains from St. Pancras and 54 chains beyond Bedford North Junction. The Bromham signal box was on the east side of the line opposite the junction between the passenger and goods lines to the south of the viaduct.

AMBERGATE STATION   Some notes by BOB ESSERY

All pictures from the author's collection unless noted otherwise.

According to the late David Tee, whose notes are on the reverse of the print, this was Ambergate on Saturday, 2nd August 1941. The passenger train was probably the 1.4 p.m. Ambergate to Sheffield and the signals had been pulled off for the 12.13 p.m. Derby to Chesterfield. He also recorded that at this date the engine was allocated to Peterborough and that although the engine was carrying a 1940 boiler, it still retained a tall dome casing. Finally, he also drew my attention to the partial blackout on the station lamps.   H. C. CASSERLEY

A panoramic view of Ambergate taken c.1910 looking north towards Manchester with a London St. Pancras to Manchester express in the distance.

THE triangular station and junctions at Ambergate, on the old Midland Railway line, were in a valley some 10½ miles north of Derby, in the County of Derbyshire. Ambergate is the southern end of the Peak District, an area of outstanding beauty, and when all the lines that radiated from the station were open, it would have been a remarkable place to watch trains. My footplate recollections were limited and, sadly, I did not realize the importance of the junction until some years after I left railway service.

The first station at Ambergate was opened in 1840 on the old North Midland Railway, which was one of the three constituent companies that, following amalgamation in 1844, became the Midland Railway. The first station building was where the goods shed is shown on the station diagram reproduced here. It was on the original line from Derby to Leeds and the North. After crossing the River Derwent, this line went through Toadmoor Tunnel before reaching the station. Fortunately, an engraving of the original station has survived and is reproduced here. Later, after the third station was opened, the original line was used as a direct road from Derby to the North (and vice versa), for trains that did not call at Ambergate station, and my footplate experiences at Ambergate were only over this section of railway.

In 1848 a further section of line was made on the north side of the first station, called the Manchester, Buxton, Matlock & Midland Junction Railway. This was opened in 1848 from Ambergate to Rowsley and gave a through road from the North to Rowsley, which was extended to Hassop in 1862, and Buxton in 1863. With the further extension from Miller's Dale Junction to Manchester opened in 1866 for goods trains, and 1867 for passenger trains, it completed the old Midland Railway main line from London St. Pancras to Manchester.

The second station was opened in 1863 and although it was replaced by the third station in 1876, the buildings remained in use for many years and are shown on p. 60. At the same

This copy of an engraving by S. Russell shows the original station at Ambergate.

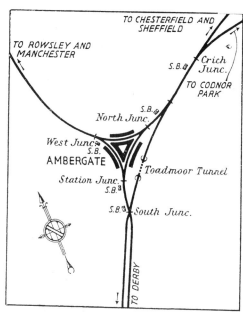

A simplified diagram originally published in the Railway Gazette in 1936, to show the position of the various signal boxes in the area.

time, a section of line was laid in, leading from the north line (see diagram), at the south end of the then new station, and connecting at the west end with the Rowsley line previously mentioned; this gave a through line from Derby to Buxton, and four years later to Manchester. In 1876, when the third station was built, another junction was made connecting with the north line about 150 yards on the north side of the first station, and with the Manchester line at the south end of the station, thus completing the triangle shown on the diagram.

The station was in a valley and it was built on stone supports about 33ft above the public road. The six platforms were built on the same level, and were accessible to one another by level crossings, while a footbridge at the south end of the station connected platforms 1, 2, 3 and 4. The public road passed under all the platforms. In addition to the Derwent, the railway passed over the River Amber on the west side of the station.

Cottages for railway employees were built between the main line to the north and No. 4 platform (see diagram) and a dock was built near the south end of No. 4 platform for unloading horses and vehicles. This enabled them to be detached from

SHEET 14.

This is part of page 13D of the third edition 1920 of the Midland Railway Distance Diagrams and has been included to show a detailed enlargement of the Ambergate area

Centre of Sidings 141ᵐ79ᶜ (142ᵐ52ᶜ)
Shirland Colliery Branch Junction 141ᵐ77ᶜ via Heanor (142ᵐ50ᶜ via Belper)

To Leeds

WINGFIELD 141ᵐ11ᶜ (141ᵐ64ᶜ)
Station S.B.141ᵐ4ᶜ (141ᵐ57ᶜ)
End of M.R. 141ᵐ14ᶜ (141ᵐ67ᶜ)
Junction 140ᵐ78ᶜ (141ᵐ51ᶜ)

OAKERTHORPE OR SOUTH WINGFIELD COLLIERY

OAKERTHORPE

SOUTH WINGFIELD

Wingfield Manor

SWANWICK COLLIERY

RIVER NORTH MIDLAND AMBER

CRICH STAND

LIME STONE QUARRIES

Amber Bridge Nº54. (140ᵐ40ᶜ)

SWANWICK

WHATSTANDWELL
PASS: 140ᵐ13ᶜ (140ᵐ13ᶜ)

From Manchester

CRICH

LIME STONE QUARRIES

FRITCHLEY

(THE CLAY CROSS COY.)

(THE BUTTERLEY COY.)

TRAMWAY

CRICH CHASE

CROMFORD

AMBERGATE RIVER DERWENT AND ROWSLEY M.R.

CANAL

BULL BRIDGE

North End (139ᵐ59ᶜ)
WINGFIELD TUNNEL Nº81: 260 YARDS
South End (139ᵐ47ᶜ)

Buckland Hollow
(0ᵐ0ᶜ Branch Mileage)

Ambergate or Bull Bridge Brick Works 137ᵐ50ᶜ (138ᵐ24ᶜ)
Buckland Hollow Branch Junction 137ᵐ3ᶜ (137ᵐ57ᶜ)
Buckland Hollow S.B.137ᵐ1ᶜ (137ᵐ55ᶜ)
Cromford Canal Bridge Nº6. (137ᵐ38ᶜ)

PENTRICH

Pentrich Colliery Sidings 136ᵐ7ᶜ (136ᵐ60ᶜ)
S.B. 136ᵐ6ᶜ 156ᵐ61ᶜ
End of M.R. 136ᵐ91ᶜ

PENTRICH COLLIERY

BUTTERLEY JUNCTION
Butterley Reservoir Viaduct via Codnor Pk
Butterley Junction S.B. (136ᵐ5ᶜ)
Butterley Junction (136ᵐ4ᶜ via Codnor Pk)

BUTTERLEY
Station S.B. (135ᵐ...
M. R.

48ᶜ

Butterley Junction 135ᵐ30ᶜ
Butterley Junction S.B.(135ᵐ29ᶜ)
Viaduct Nº1 (135ᵐ18ᶜ)
Bridge Nº77 (135ᵐ6ᶜ)

M.R. AND HEANOR 1ᵐ15ᶜ

RIPLEY

West Junction 138ᵐ26ᶜ (138ᵐ26ᶜ)
STATION 138ᵐ18ᶜ (138ᵐ18ᶜ)
Station Junction 138ᵐ10ᶜ (138ᵐ10ᶜ)

Crich Junction (138ᵐ56ᶜ via Codnor Park)
(138ᵐ55ᶜ via Belper)
138ᵐ2ᶜ via Heanor

North Junction (138ᵐ30ᶜ via Belper)
138ᵐ27ᶜ via Heanor

RIDGEWAY

NETHER HEAGE

LOWER HARTSHAY

CROMFORD M.R. CANAL

BUCKLAND HOLLOW BRANCH

AMBERGATE
SEE ENLARGEMENT

The Duke of Devonshire's Wharf (0ᵐ...)

South Junction 137ᵐ74ᶜ (137ᵐ74ᶜ)

(SEE SHEET 67)

BUTTERLEY COY'S LINE

HARTSHAY COLLIERY

RIPLEY
Station Loop Nº...
STATION 134...

Derwent Bridge Nº39. (137ᵐ5ᶜ)

JOHNSON'S SIDINGS 138ᵐ68ᶜ (138ᵐ68ᶜ)
JOHNSON'S SIDING S.B. (138ᵐ66ᶜ)

HORSLEY

BROADHOLM

Derwent Bridge Nº37. (136ᵐ44ᶜ)
Broadholme S.B. (136ᵐ33ᶜ)

Derwent Bridge Nº36. (136ᵐ14ᶜ)

RIVER

PASSENGER STATION 135ᵐ53ᶜ (135ᵐ53ᶜ)
Passenger Station S.B. (135ᵐ48ᶜ)

BELPER

DERWE...

White MOO...

AMBERGATE.

FROM MANCHESTER

WEST JUNCTION

North Junction 138ᵐ33ᶜ
North Junction (138ᵐ31ᶜ via Station)
Curve Junction (0ᵐ9ᶜ)
STATION (0ᵐ1ᶜ)
(138ᵐ17ᶜ)

North Junction S.B. (0ᵐ7ᶜ)
North Junction (0ᵐ2ᶜ)
(138ᵐ16ᶜ)

RIVER DERWENT

WEST JUNCTION
West Junction 138ᵐ26ᶜ (138ᵐ26ᶜ)
S.B. (138ᵐ25ᶜ)
STATION 138ᵐ18ᶜ (138ᵐ18ᶜ)
Station Junction & S.B. 138ᵐ10ᶜ (138ᵐ10ᶜ)
STATION JUNCTION

South Junction S.B.(137ᵐ76ᶜ)
South Junction (137ᵐ74ᶜ)
137ᵐ74ᶜ

CROMFORD CANAL

To Pye...
RIVER AMBER Bull Bri...

Cromford Canal

Crich Junction
Glossop's Siding
Crich Junction S.B.
Crich Junction (138ᵐ56ᶜ via Codnor Park)
(138ᵐ55ᶜ via Belper)
(138ᵐ2ᶜ via Heanor)

End of M.R. (138ᵐ56ᶜ)

The Devonshire County Council Siding
& Glossop's Siding 138ᵐ...

AMBERGATE LINE WORKS (CLAY CROSS COY.)

MIDLAND

Junction (138ᵐ30ᶜ via Belper)
(138ᵐ28ᶜ via Heanor)

North Junction 138ᵐ33ᶜ
(138ᵐ31ᶜ via Station)

STATION 138ᵐ19ᶜ (138ᵐ19ᶜ)
North Junction S.B. (138ᵐ19ᶜ)
North End (138ᵐ13ᶜ)
South End (138ᵐ7ᶜ)
TOADMOOR TUNNEL Nº44: 129 YARDS

SOUTH JUNCTION
South Junction (137ᵐ74ᶜ)
South Junction S.B. (137ᵐ76ᶜ)
South Junction 137ᵐ74ᶜ (137ᵐ74ᶜ)
Derwent Bridge Nº42. (137ᵐ72ᶜ)

North End (137ᵐ61ᶜ)
LONGLAND TUNNEL Nº41: 101 YARDS
South End (137ᵐ56ᶜ)

FROM DERBY

To Leeds

RAILWAY STATION AMBERGATE

This picture was taken facing north with the Leeds line to the right and the Manchester platform on the far left.

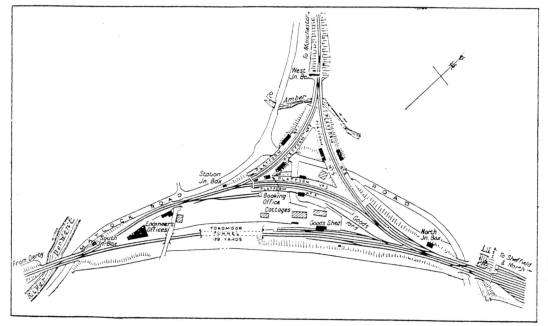

This diagram was originally reproduced in the LMS Magazine *and shows the Ambergate station area.*

the up Manchester or up North trains without difficulty. As will be seen by the diagram, a train could be completely turned by simply running it round the triangle; this was done several times daily. The connection to the goods yard was from the down north main line. Just beyond the junction, on the north side, were some marshalling sidings and private sidings serving Bull Bridge Lime Works and Glossop's siding. There was another private siding, Johnson's siding, on the Manchester line.

Triangular junctions on main-line routes are not very common and they provided some interesting operational features. Ambergate was the junction between two important trunk routes (from Derby to Rowsley and Manchester, and to Chesterfield, Sheffield, and Leeds). It was a key-point in the punctual working for both passengers and freight. The frequent passenger services using these routes included many important main-line expresses whilst there was heavy freight traffic between Chaddesden (Derby) and either Rowsley sidings or Clay Cross, together with many inter-district trains. In addition, there were heavy freight movements from Rowsley to the Toton direction over the Ambergate to Codnor Park line, which diverged from the west-to-

north route at Crich Junction. This route was also used by Nottingham to Manchester Central expresses and by a local passenger service; in the summer it was employed for through trains between the Midlands and Blackpool.

The accompanying diagrams and sketch maps show the arrangement of lines at Ambergate, together with the five signal boxes concerned. All the lines shown were double with the exception of the section from Broadholme (on the Derby line) to Ambergate south junction, between which points there were four running roads. Punctual working over such a series of junctions called for a high

TRIANGULAR RAILWAY STATION, AM

Another undated, but Edwardian view of the station taken from the footbridge seen in the picture on page 52.

It is not possible to positively identify the stock number of the Compound that was working an Up Manchester Central to London St. Pancras express passenger train in August 1928 when it was assisted by 2–4–0 No. 240.

standard of efficiency and accuracy of judgment on the part of the signal-men, since any train traversing the area was bound to prevent one or more other movements being made over the various conflicting junctions. A train from the Codnor Park line to Rowsley, for instance, had to traverse three junctions, and a train from Rowsley to Derby three.

Ambergate North Junction box was a reporting point for control purposes, acting as a liaison for the other boxes in respect of movements with which the North Junction itself was not concerned, and, owing to the many shunting movements to and from the up and down sidings and yard, the work required a high degree of efficiency at Ambergate. The South Junction box was the only one to be affected by all movements between Derby and both the Sheffield and the Manchester lines; consequently, it handled the largest number of trains (1,186 in a typical working week of the winter service, with a maximum of 75 in one eight-hour period) of any of the five boxes. Moreover, there were two up and two

down roads between South Junction box and Broadholme (the nearest signal box in the Derby direction), and when traffic was very heavy, the discrimination of the signalmen in arranging the routeing of trains on either the fast or the slow line to or from Broadholme had an important effect on the smooth flow of traffic through Ambergate. The five Ambergate signal boxes were: Ambergate South Junction (45 working levers); Ambergate Station Junction (16 working levers); Ambergate West Junction (15 working levers); Ambergate North Junction (44 working levers); and Crich Junction (30 working levers).

Although the Manchester line is no more, the beautiful scenery of Derbyshire remains, as does the line of the North Midland Railway. I hope that those readers who may be familiar with the area will agree with me when I say that this is an area well worth visiting.

This 1976 picture shows the arch spanning the A6 road below the platform for the Manchester line.

D. IBBOTSON

This 1930s view shows Ambergate south junction with an express hauled by two 4–4–0s. No. 531 was the train engine and No. 424 the pilot. Reference to the diagram on page 54 will show the position the train was crossing the Matlock Road, and the second station, now the Engineer's offices, can be seen in the background.

This April 1939 view shows part of the second Ambergate station buildings and forecourt. The Engineer's Department used the buildings as offices and their position can be seen on the station diagram.

This shows the south end of Toadmoor Tunnel, which was 129 yards in length.

This shows Class 4F No. 44168 passing Ambergate in April 1957 with an Up train of empty coal wagons running under Class H Through Freight train headlamp code. Note than when compared with earlier pictures, both running lines now had check rails.
FRANK ASHLEY

Taken from the carriage window, this shows No. 44380 hauling a Matlock to Derby Ordinary Passenger train on 3rd September 1939 and a glimpse of the station Junction signal box to the extreme right.

R. M. CASSERLEY

This is another view of the footbridge seen in the photo on page 52. In his notes on the reverse of the print, the late Dave Ibbotson draws attention to the barrow crossing and the two different types of lamps on the footbridge. The locomotive, Patriot Class 4–6–0 No. 45509, was at the head of a Down Ordinary Passenger train on the Manchester line.

D. IBBOTSON

This picture, taken on 3rd September 1955 from the window of a Nottingham to Matlock excursion train, shows the north curve platforms, which at this part of the station were of wood construction.
R. M. CASSERLEY

This undated picture shows Crich Junction (see diagram on page 53), looking south towards Ambergate North Junction.

AUSTIN MOTOR WORKS, LONGBRIDGE

Notes by BOB ESSERY

In 1950, when I completed my National Service, I returned to the railway at Saltley Motive Power Depot and found that my seniority placed me in the Trip Link. For the benefit of readers who may be unfamiliar with the question of seniority and links, it should be explained that promotion for firemen and drivers was not identical. At Saltley, firemen went from link to link in what was an upwards progression, starting with the Washwood Heath Link, which covered most but not all local steam shunting turns, and all shed work. From the Washwood Heath line they progressed into the Bank Pilots, Control, Special and Trip link before going into one of the bottom group of road links. When I went into the Army, I was in the Control link, but due to military service, I did not complete my time in

the Control link and I missed the Special link, returning to find that my mate was Freddie Robinson, a senior driver, who, because he was diabetic, had applied for a vacancy in the Trip link, where the work was less demanding than many of the jobs in either of the two groups of freight road links or the various passenger links. In fact, all the drivers in the Trip link were there because of medical reasons.

All the work was within the Birmingham area and we had about two weeks work in twelve on the Halesowen branch, where I encountered the unusual sight of privately owned locomotives hauling trains over railway company lines. Unfortunately, this was at a time when my interest in railways did not go as deep as it should, so although I clearly recall seeing Austin locomotives running over

This short wheelbase 0—6—0 saddle tank, photographed at Longbridge on 5th May 1962, was named Abernant *and built by Manning Wardle in 1921.*
T. J. EDGINGTON

This picture was taken at Longbridge, probably in 1962, and shows another short wheelbase 0—6—0 saddle tank that was built in 1932 by Kitson of Leeds. The locomotive carried the name Austin I, but unfortunately I do not have any other information.
T. J. EDGINGTON

Taken at Longbridge on 5th May 1962, this picture shows Vulcan, which was built by W. G. Bagnall in 1950. The locomotive was in very good condition and appears to have just been repainted.
T. J. EDGINGTON

This is another picture that was taken at Longbridge on 5th May 1962, which shows Austin II. This locomotive was built in 1936 by the Hunslet Engine Company. Note that all these locomotives carried only one lamp holder that was either on the front of the smokebox or at the base of the chimney.   T. J. EDGINGTON

railway company lines, I failed to ask how this was allowed. Therefore this short feature is in part designed to place this information on record by asking readers if they can fill in some of the gaps in the Austin story and to generally enlarge upon the practice of privately owned locomotives and trains running over railway company lines.

I assume that every locomotive would have to be registered with the railway company and be subject to some form of inspection on a regular basis. The drivers, and probably the firemen, would have to be passed out by the railway inspectors as being conversant with the

railway company rules, which prior to Nationalisation on this joint line, were those of the old LMS Company. No doubt there were local instructions in respect of these workings but I have never found any documentary evidence about the subject, so, rather than leave the story untold, I have published what I know as a postscript to Roger Carpenter's two-part article on the line that was published in *Midland Record* Nos. 23 & 24.

I cannot recall the colour used to paint the Austin Motor Company's locomotives, but fortunately John Edgington, whose pictures have been used here, was able to confirm that it was green with yellow lining.

This picture, taken at the Halesowen Junction end of Longbridge station, shows Austin No. 5, with its train emerging from below the bridge that carried the Bristol Road South over the Joint line. Although the other pictures show Austin locomotives at Longbridge, this view illustrates a privately owned locomotive running over railway company lines as mentioned in the text. No. 5 was built in 1943 by the Davenport Locomotive Works, Iowa, USA.
P. B. WHITEHOUSE

The Austin Motor Works owned a number of rail wagons and this picture shows a 12-ton steel mineral wagon that was built for the company by Charles Roberts in 1928.
WAKEFIELD COLLECTION

MIDLAND TERRITORY

Bulwell in Nottinghamshire lay between Basford Junction and Hucknall on the Nottingham & Mansfield line and was opened on 2nd October 1848. The period one (the Signalling Record Society's classification) signal box, just visible to the left of the picture, was raised in height on 25th June 1899, being replaced by a new signal box which opened on 11th September 1927. In this 3rd April 1922 picture we see a group of workmen together with two Company servants. Note the absence of a passenger footbridge; all persons wishing to cross the running lines would need to use the barrow crossing, and no doubt the notice, the back of which can be seen on the right of the picture, provided the official warning.
NATIONAL RAILWAY MUSEUM (DY 12489)

The J. S. Moore Affair

by GRAHAM WARBURTON

This is an account of a personality clash and a grievance between W. C. Acfield, H. E. Morgan and J. S. Moore following the transfer of the latter from the London Tilbury & Southend Railway to the Midland Railway Signal Department at Derby, after the LT&SR became part of the Midland Railway, which ultimately led to his redundancy from the LMS Railway. The story concludes with an interesting twist to the tale.

James Samuel Moore was born on 6th March 1863 in Abbey Street, Derby, the son of James and Martha Moore (formerly Smith). His father was a Staff Sergeant in the Derby Militia. The 1881 census records him aged 18 residing at 5 Oakfield Terrace, Childer Thornton, Cheshire, where he was a carpenter working on the Great Western Railway erecting signal boxes.

On 26th December 1889 (aged 26 and stated to be a carpenter) he married Elizabeth Irvine, a widow aged 24 living at 20 George Street (Cheetham Hill), Manchester, in St. Mark's Parish Church, Cheetham Hill. The 1901 census reveals him to be living at 166 London Road, Grays, Thurrock, by which time he had three daughters and a son. His occupation was now a Railway Signal Engineer employed by the London Tilbury & Southend Railway.

For an account of the career of this brilliant signal engineer we can do no better than refer to the obituary that appeared in the Institution of Railway Signal Engineers Proceedings in 1951, which was extracted from his article in the IRSE Proceedings for 1943 entitled 'Some Recollections' referred to below.

James Samuel Moore commenced his railway career at Derby in 1877 in the office of the Chief Accountant, of the Midland Railway, William Henry Hodges. In the following year he entered the service of Saxby and Farmer as an improver, engaged on the erection of signal boxes on the Great Western Railway at Warwick

James Samuel Moore 1863-1950.

and Birmingham. He then proceeded to Shrewsbury, Birkenhead, Wolverhampton and Chipping Norton. In 1884 he left Saxby and Farmer, taking a post with the Railway Signal Company, Liverpool, where he was engaged on work for that firm at Hereford and then at Victoria Station, Manchester, on the Lancashire and Yorkshire Railway. From there he went to Ireland to erect a number of installations on the Great Southern and Western Railway before returning to England to do similar work on the Mersey Railway and at Gravesend on the London, Chatham and Dover Railway. In 1886 he was again working in Liverpool at the Exchange Station. After that, as foreman, he had charge of installing point detectors at many places throughout the L&YR system. He then spent some time reorganising and improving the signalling on the Cork Bandon and South Coast Railway, before working at a number of stations on the Midland and Great Northern Joint Railway and then at

and near the Forth Bridge. This was followed by further installations on the Great Northern Railway, Cheshire Lines, Manchester, Sheffield and Lincolnshire (later Great Central) and, again in Ireland, on the Midland Great Western line.

The Railway Signal Company then had a considerable contract for the new Lancashire, Derbyshire and East Coast Railway, later absorbed by the Great Central, when Mr. Moore took charge of the work. After doing more work on the Great Central (London extension) route he was appointed Signal Inspector to the London Tilbury and Southend Railway, being practically its Signal Superintendent. A very great amount of work was carried out on that line in due course under his direction, by his old firm, not only in conjunction with the modernising of the equipment on the old portions of the railway but also on the important Bow (Campbell Road) to Barking widening following the completion of the Whitechapel and Bow Railway, which enabled trains to run through from the District Railway. Extensive alterations were made at Tilbury and nearby. On January 1st 1912 the LT&SR was absorbed by the Midland Railway and in 1915 Mr. Moore was transferred to Headquarters at Derby under Mr. W. C. Acfield with the title of Interlocking Inspector, working as an assistant to Mr. H. E. Morgan. On the latter's return, after being grievously wounded from the army, Mr. Moore became his principal assistant. Moore retired on September 5th 1925, after a particularly interesting career in mechanical signalling work, during which he had acquired a most complete knowledge of all its branches which earned him much respect among those with whom he came into contact, both in railway and industrial circles. He was responsible for several inventions, some of which met with a good deal of favour on some lines, including a compensator for Claytons fogging machine (patent No. 2062 26/1/1906,

2062. Moore, J. S. Jan. 26. 1906

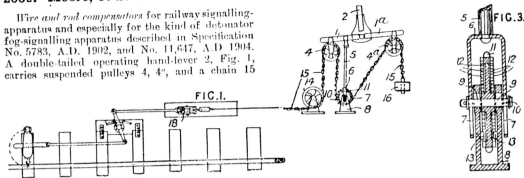

FIC.I.

FIG.3.

Wire and rod compensators for railway signalling-apparatus and especially for the kind of detonator fog-signalling apparatus described in Specification No. 5783, A.D. 1902, and No. 11,647, A.D 1904. A double-tailed operating hand-lever 2, Fig. 1, carries suspended pulleys 4, 4ᵃ, and a chain 15

passes from a balance weight 16 around the pulley 4ᵃ and over a sprocket-wheel 11, and around the pulley 4 and a guide-pulley 14 to be connected to the wire leading to a weighted bell-crank lever 18 at the detonator apparatus. The wheel 11 is carried in slotted bearings 9, Fig. 3, in a fixed standard 8, and is normally held down by a slotted stirrup 6 attached to a link 5 pivoted to the hand-lever. In this position the wheel 11 is depressed so that internal teeth 12 on it are out of engagement with teeth 13 fixed to the standard 8, and the wheel 13 is free to revolve and the balance weight 16, Fig. 1, takes up any slack in the wires. When the hand-lever is operated, raising the tail 1 and the link 5, during the first part of the motion the long slots 7, Fig. 3, in the stirrup 6 rise about the wheel spindle

10 and the released wheel 11 is raised by the pull of the balance weight 16 on the chain, and the fixed teeth 13 engage with the internal teeth 12 to fix the wheel 11. Further movement of the hand-lever is permitted by the length of the slots 7 and the chain is thereby drawn inwards to operate the detonator apparatus. A detonator may be affixed to the base of the balance weight 16 to sound an alarm in case of breakage of the chain 15 and consequent fall of the weight. In a modified form, the internal teeth in the wheel 11 may be dispensed with, and the ordinary sprocket teeth on the wheel 11 engage in its elevated position with fixed teeth formed on the underside of the standard 8, which is continued over the top of the sprocket-wheel for this purpose.

13,426. Moore, J. S. June 10. 1907

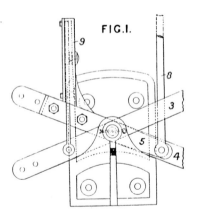

FIG.I.

Controlling and locking signals.—A mechanical slot or coacting apparatus for controlling railway signals is shown in Figs. 1 and 2, in which the two levers 3, 4 are operated from the separate controlling-cabins. The intermediate lever 5 has attached to it a vertically sliding box 9, on a spindle in which is mounted a pawl or tumbler 11. This tumbler is in the form of a quadrant having its straight sides related so that the apex 11ᵃ coincides with its axis of rotation, and is cut away at 12, 12ᵃ to provide shoulders 13, 13ᵃ at right-angles. To the levers 3, 4 are connected the slides 14, 15, provided at their upper ends with lateral projections forming shoulders 14ᵃ, 15ᵃ. When the lever 3 is pulled over, the corresponding slide 14 is pulled down, thus pushing the tumbler 11 over so that when the lever 4 is pulled over the shoulder 15ᵃ engages with the shoulder 13 of the tumbler. The box 9 is thereby pulled down, thus moving over the lever 5, and moving the signal to 'clear' through the connexion 8. When either of the levers 3, 4 is returned the tumbler rotates and allows the box 9 and the lever 5 to rise, thus returning the signal to 'danger.' An alternative arrangement is shown in Fig. 11, in which the box 9 is placed longitudinally of the lever 5, and the slides 14, 15 are pivotally connected by links 18, 19 to the levers 3, 4. Should either of the links 18, 19 become disconnected, the corresponding slide falls below the tumbler and no downward movement of the casing can be effected. The same result may be obtained in the first arrangement by lengthening the box 9, Figs. 1 and 2. The box may be fixed to any part of the lever 5, it being only necessary to rearrange the slides 14, 15 and the pawl 11 to suit the action required.

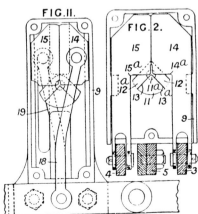

FIG.II. FIG. 2.

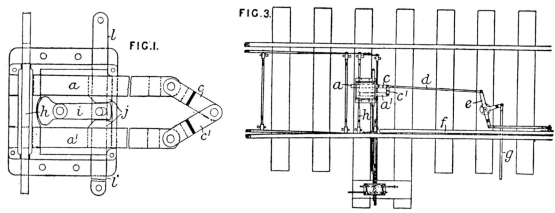

Fig. 3. Patent 23754, 17th November 1905, 'Interlocking apparatus; indicators'.

23,754. Moore, J. S. Nov. 17.

Interlocking - apparatus; indicators. — In a detector mechanism, toggle mechanism operates the two locking-bolts, which have a further motion beyond the locking-motion to release the signal, a further pair of sliding bolts being combined with the apparatus to control electric circuits indicating that the points are exactly in place. The locking-bolts a, a^1, Figs. 1 and 3, are actuated by toggles c, c^1 through a rod d and a T-lever e connected to the ordinary locking-bar f and the connexion g to the cabin. According to the position of the points, one inoperative bar a or a^1 forms the fulcrum for the toggles to move the other bar a^1 or a through the locking-notch in the stretcher bar h. The continued movement of the bar a or a^1 causes a projection j, Fig. 1, to turn a pivoted lever i, and actuate a sliding bar l connected with the signal-locking or detector slide. Additional sliding bars m, m^1, Fig. 5, connected each with a point tongue carry a lever n pivoted at o, o^1 on each bar. Relative movement of the tongues will cause rotation of the lever n, and thereby break an indicating-circuit at contacts p, p^1 closed by the lever n.

Fig. 4. Patent 10712, 7th May 1906, 'Interlocking apparatus; indicators'.

10,712. Moore, J. S. May 7 1906

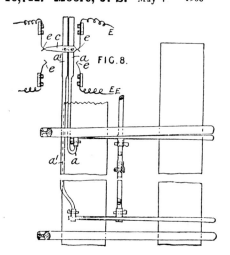

Interlocking-apparatus; indicators.—In a point detector mechanism, which electrically or mechanically detects relative movement of the two point tongues, two slides a, a^1 are connected each to a tongue and are arranged to be parallel and close together. A pin on each tongue engages in a slot in a lever c, so that relative movement of the tongues causes the lever c to turn on either pin as fulcrum, and the end of the lever c magnifies the movement. Such movement may be communicated mechanically to the signal locking slides, or the lever c may normally close, through contacts e, a circuit E to the signal cabin, and this circuit is broken if the lever c is rotated. The arrangement may be used in combination with the locking-plungers of facing point locks, or with the point-locking mechanism described in Specification No. 23,754, A.D. 1905. The slides a, a^1 may be arranged between the rails, instead of at one side as shown.

Fig. 1) and a push-off type tappet action signal slot (patent No. 13426, 10/6/1907, Fig. 2) which was used on Tilbury and Great Eastern lines. He also patented and made a duplex type facing point lock, (patent No. 23754 17/11/1905, Fig. 3) which was first introduced at the Tilbury East Junction signal box in 1906.

In addition Moore took out a further patent No. 10712 (7/5/1906 Fig. 4) covering 'Interlocking-apparatus; indicators' that could be used in conjunction with patent 23754 above. Elected an Associate Member of the Institution in 1913 and a Full Member in 1922, Mr. Moore read to it a paper on the theory of interlocking, on which he was an acknowledged authority, which awoke considerable discussion. He presented the slides used with it to the Institution. In 1943 when there was much difficulty in finding material for the journal, he provided an interesting contribution to it, detailing a number of his recollections. His facing point lock was illustrated in the issue for that year. He was thought by some to have been the first to apply switch-extension pieces for actuating the detector rods and Mr. R. S. Griffiths, in his history of the development of facing point protection, published in the Proceedings for 1936/7, supported this claim.

James Samuel Moore was clearly a very accomplished signal engineer, and what now follows is an account of Moore's career and frustrations following the acquisition of The London Tilbury & Southend Railway by the Midland Railway in 1912 as recounted by John Sadler.

The Signalling Superintendent or Signalling Inspector, as he was called on the LTSR, was James Samuel Moore who was an ex employee of the Railway Signal Company (RS.Co) of Fazakerley, Liverpool. The RSCo. had many contracts on the LTSR, and when the civil engineer of the line, Mr. James Robertson, requested the RSCo to provide an officer or agent to take responsibility for the maintenance and execution of future work, they had no hesitation in recommending their servant James Samuel Moore, who was duly transferred on 22nd July 1897. Moore then established a District HQ at Grays in Essex where offices were established in that town, the District becoming Grays District.

In the year 1912 the Midland Railway acquired control and responsibility for the London Tilbury and Southend Railway whose line extended from Campbell Road Junction to Barking and thence into Essex on the north bank of the River Thames. In March 1913 the Midland Railway Signal Superintendent, W. C. Acfield,

525

Moore's Slot (Railway Signal Co. Catalogue, page 32).

became responsible for the maintenance and construction of signalling on the LTSR line.

Acfield took great interest in his newly acquired responsibility, as being a Londoner, and former partner in the Company of Saxby and Farmer, he was well acquainted with traffic conditions and signalling in the London area. Acfield took an early opportunity to meet Moore at Grays, and it seems that right from the start they did not get on particularly well together, one reason being that Acfield was aware that Moore was receiving royalties from some of his signalling equipment patents used on the line. One particular invention was the 'Moore Patent Signalling Slot' (*Fig. 1*), manufactured under licence by the RS Co. It had been noticed at Derby, when plans of the LTSR signalling became available, the large number of signals which were slotted.

Acfield advised Moore that the MR did not pay royalties to any of its servants, which obviously upset Moore and led to poor relations between them right from the start. (Notwithstanding, it is worth mentioning that Midland Railway minute 5610 dated 21st October 1892 approved the royalty payment of £1028 to A. A. Langley for the installation of 1028 'Langley and Prince' facing point locks which he had jointly patented with Prince on 14th December 1886 – No. 1640.)

On 1st January 1911 Herbert Edward Morgan had joined the MR from the W. R. Sykes Interlocking Co., and following experience in the Derby D.O., and also as District Inspector at Appleby, he was appointed to the second position in the Signalling Department, known as The Chief Inspectorship of Signals. He succeeded the previous officer Mr. Robinson. Morgan, who had had experience with the Sykes Co. and also The Westinghouse Co., was trained in up-to-date practices on the busy lines in the London area in which he had worked.

Initially Morgan was not satisfied with the organization at Derby, as in his office he had an assistant, a subinspector by the name of Charles Baker, who previously had been

Inspector on the Peterborough District, which was subsequently abandoned, and with Baker's experience being limited and his reliability questioned, Morgan was anxious to find someone who would take more responsibility. On his advice Acfield appointed Moore to this position and so Moore left Grays in 1915, taking up residence in Derby, becoming sub-inspector, which later became locking inspector, with responsibility to Morgan.

In 1916 Morgan joined the Forces to take charge of mechanical signalling on the French and Belgium railways in the area of the British Expeditionary Force and Moore was detailed to deputize for him in his absence. Therefore, until the return of Morgan in 1922, Moore had the responsibility for the detailed signalling works with particular regard to schemes and interlocking work outside on the line. Moore was very happy in this capacity and was thought well of by his staff and by

everyone with whom he came in contact. He was a distinguished man with a goaty beard, always immaculately dressed and had very much the appearance of H.M. King George V.

His greatest asset was his knowledge and high regard for interlocking work, and he made great friends with everyone outside, particularly fitters in the works, helping them with interlocking theory, and the compilation and arrangement of the interlocking amongst the levers within signalling frames.

One feature of the MR signalling practice was, that when a frame had been erected, and was ready for dismantling, it was tested to ensure that the execution of the interlocking was satisfactorily performed and was in accordance with what was required for traffic purposes. To achieve this an inspector or qualified person was always detailed to test over the frame by working the levers to a signalling diagram before the frame was dismantled. Moore carried out this duty

assiduously as often as he could, but in his absence, his assistant, Baker, carried it out.

In 1922 Morgan was demobilized, and, on returning to his normal duties, he was appointed as Chief Assistant to the Signal Superintendent who was Acfield, with Moore appointed as Signalling Inspector with responsibility to Morgan, which upset Moore who never settled down happily in this position. When on the Tilbury line, he was solely responsible to his Chief Engineer and resented having to report his actions to Morgan, who was Acfield's deputy, and it is this that started the ill-feeling on Moore's part.

In April 1919, the lever frame in the large signal box at Morecambe Promenade containing 92 levers was replaced by a standard MR tappet frame. John Sadler was sent by Acfield to work on the installation of this frame in the signal box, requiring the removal of the tumbler frame at the back of the box and erecting a

Wilfred Cosens Acfield – Signal Superintendent Midland Railway from 1st February 1905 to the grouping and LMS Divisional Signal and Telegraph Derby and Crewe, retiring on 25th August 1927.

Herbert Edward Morgan joined the Midland Railway on 1st January 1911 and retired as LMS Divisional Signal and Telegraph Engineer Crewe in 1948.

Morecambe Promenade signal box where J. S. Moore found the 1906 tumbler locking unsatisfactory when it was replaced with a tappet frame in 1919.

The interior of Morecambe Promenade signal box, showing the original Midland tumbler frame at the rear of the box.

new tappet frame on the window side of the signal box.

When the work was completed Moore came along to test the interlocking with the assistance of Mr. A. J. Fossey, the sub-inspector from Skipton, who pulled the levers together with Sadler. When the work was completed, Moore enquired of Sadler as to whether he was interested in the theory of interlocking. Sadler obviously was and they immediately sat down and discussed interlocking problems in general. Sadler was fascinated and impressed by the way Moore handled the matter, as in those days the compilation of interlocking was somewhat of a mystery.

Moore was very critical of MR signalling, and, having heard that this particular installation was Acfield's first important work on joining the Midland Railway, made a point of visiting Morecambe to test the locking thoroughly. In so doing, Moore was able to force some of the levers against the interlocking and was actually able to clear signals with the route blocked on account of the position of other levers. This was a serious fault, because it meant that it was possible to signal clear routes that were actually blocked by points being in the wrong position. On reporting this to Acfield, one can only imagine the effect this had on the mutual feelings between the two officers.

It was a serious matter and the frame had to be altered and a new one built. The reason for this state of affairs appeared to have been a weakness in the old MR type of tumbler locking by which it was possible, under certain conditions, to put so much strain on the gear that a springing or slackness could be caused which would enable a lever, which should have been locked, to have been worked as it should not have been.

This was a fundamental fault of this system and one of the primary reasons why, on his arrival at Derby, Acfield had attempted to design a frame with tappet locking. Moore concluded the talk in the signal box by sarcastically saying 'It wasn't much of a tribute to Mr. Acfield's early work at Derby, was it?', following this by adding 'You know in sig-

nalling work and interlocking the MR are 30 years behind the times and things should have been tackled long before this'. It is not surprising that relations between Moore and Acfield became somewhat estranged. In spite of this, Moore was always very helpful and courteous in dealing with D.O. and office personnel. Moore was obviously very unhappy in the situation in which he found himself, resenting being compelled to report to Mr. Morgan as his superior. Not surprisingly, he sought to have his position clarified and be given the independence to which he thought he was entitled.

Firstly, he complained strongly to Acfield, requesting some redress, but apparently Acfield was either unable or unwilling to concede, and on this account it became known that Moore had written privately to the Divisional Civil Engineer, Mr. H. P. Miles, setting out the facts of his complaint. Moore saw Miles privately but without getting any satisfaction.

On 1st January 1923 the MR had become part of the LMS group associated with the LNWR, L&Y and other railways, and, of this combination, Mr. Trench of the LNWR was appointed Chief Civil Engineer. With a view to having his position rectified or adjusted, Moore then wrote privately to Trench complaining about his position.

His case was, that having been the Chief Officer for signalling on the LTS, he had been brought to Derby with every vestige of authority taken away from him and had been put solely under the control of Mr. Morgan, who he regarded as being insufficiently qualified or experienced to assume this control over him. He privately accused Mr. Morgan of arrogance and indifference in getting out on to the line to make tests and inspections. In this he was rather unfair to Morgan as he had been severely wounded while in the Forces, having lost a leg below the knee, and, although Morgan was plucky and willing, and did his best, he suffered somewhat from this disability when it would have been reasonable to expect to receive all the assistance in this matter from Moore.

Unfortunately, Moore regarded this position as inefficiency or unsat-

isfactory on Morgan's part and it appears that all these facts were put in writing in his complaint to Trench. Following this complaint, he was ordered to Euston for interview and, of course, expected to see Mr. Trench personally, but this was not achieved as he saw Trench's staff assistant Commander F. J. Paice who had been appointed to that position in 1913.

In this same year, 1923, he had been invited to read a paper on interlocking before the Institution of Railway Signal Engineers, which he did, but as he was in the throes of this trouble with Acfield and Trench, his nerve began to be affected and he told John Sadler, that, should he not be in the right frame of mind to read the paper himself, he would request John to do it, which, as things were, was somewhat unsettling as Sadler was reluctant to become involved in such a controversial matter. Fortunately, Moore was able to read his paper, which he did on 18th July 1923, but it was given out from Acfield's office, that, as things were, it would be regarded in disfavour for anyone from the Derby Office to attend the reading of the paper, and no-one did. On his return from reading the paper, Sadler enquired as to how to things went, to which Moore replied, 'Splendidly, the boycott really buoyed me up'.

It was a very good paper, the finest account of interlocking Sadler had ever seen, and throughout his career he always used Moore's paper as a reference and as a medium for apprentices, trainees and staff lectures. The IRSE awarded a prize to the reader of the paper adjudged to be the most valuable as decided by a specially appointed committee, and for the year 1923, Moore's paper received the prize, which was really a blow to Acfield.

Things went from bad to worse and relations between Moore and Morgan and Acfield became most strained with Moore stating that weeks went by without his seeing Acfield personally, and Morgan and Moore rarely spoke. Moore was expected to enter into a book in the office, his appointments and places of visit on the line, should Morgan wish to communicate with him for any purpose. On occasions Moore would bring Sadler the book and advise him where he was going, leaving Sadler to fill in the particulars, as he would not do so himself. Difficult as the matter was, Sadler saw no objection to this and did it regularly.

Beyond this, Moore appeared to get no further and received no satisfaction. One morning in the train from Nottingham to Derby, Sadler encountered one of the clerks from the Divisional Civil Engineers office, who raised the point of signal inspector Moore and talked about him. It was a well-known talking point and both agreed how regrettable it was, particularly following the new amalgamation of the railways, that all this 'dirty linen' was being washed in public at Euston by LNW officials. Sadler responded by agreeing, stating that he hoped it would all blow over and that things would settle down and nothing more would be heard. The response was 'Ah – but he's done something worse now – he's written to the General Manager'.

He had written a personal note, enclosing a dossier, to the General Manager of the LMS, Mr. H. G. Burgess. Very soon after this, it was given out that Moore's position as Interlocking Inspector had been abolished and therefore he would become redundant, retiring in 1925, aged 62. Tom Guest, who was the leading draughtsman in the D.O. on mechanical signalling work, was then transferred to Morgan's office to do Moore's work.

On 31st March 1927 H. G. Burgess retired from the position of General Manager and Sir Josiah Stamp received the appointment as President of the Executive Committee. This was the first appointment on any railway in this country of that title. This led to a considerable change in the organization of the railway, which included four Vice Presidents responsible for the different facets of the operation. The Vice President in charge of engineering services was Robert White Reid, previously the carriage and wagon superintendent of the LMS.

Following the railway amalgamations, no chief appointment was made for signal work, except in Scotland, where Leonard P. Lewis (who had been assistant to Stevens, the Caledonian Railway Signal Superintendent), was appointed Signal Superintendent for Scotland on Stevens' retirement. No appointment was made to the three English Divisions; Acfield remained at Derby, Roberts at Crewe and Berry at Manchester. On 30th June 1927 Roberts retired from Crewe with Acfield retiring from the Derby appointment on 25th August, also in 1927. Gossip reasonably expected that Morgan would be appointed Divisional Officer in charge of signalling at Derby, but strangely the appointments at Crewe and Derby were reversed, Oldham from Crewe was appointed to Derby and Morgan was sent to Crewe on 1st May 1928.

Morgan told Sadler that he had not heard the last of Moore, as every Christmas he received an unpleasant postcard, and, although he never revealed the details of what was said, it was apparently unpleasant, with spiteful references to the past state of affairs between them.

About this time a further complication occurred, as prior to WW1, a sensational publication appeared weekly called *John Bull*, a paper of general interest containing articles and letters from the public in general on a wide range of matters, edited by Horatio Bottomley, a well-known character in politics. During the war it was a medium for soldiers or any person with a grievance to vent their feelings by having a letter printed therein. Following the war, Bottomley became involved in some financial controversy, and his paper *John Bull* became defunct. Later, Bottomley introduced another publication entitled *John Blunt*, a sensational and even more lurid paper than the original *John Bull*, when again, any person with an axe to grind, would place an article or letter in his paper, the first issue being published on 9th February 1929.

In the *John Blunt* issue dated 16th February 1929 there was an article written by Moore entitled 'Our Death Trap Railways', containing a sketch of an unnamed junction showing signals and points, explaining that conflicting routes could be set up. He further referred to Nottingham East and Whitehall Junction, Leeds, where, when in practice, Moore had tested the levers in these frames and found that he was able to set up conflicting routes, and that, on reporting the matter to his chief officer, complications arose resulting in him being retired two years later. He also mentioned the Ashchurch collision, asserting that some of the evidence was incorrect – the article is reproduced here.

The issue dated 2nd March 1929 carried a second article, this time entitled 'Murder on the Line', giving a further sketch of a similar situation at Duffield Station, explaining again that levers had been found which could be pulled over in the frame which should have been locked, asserting that this situation had been in existence for forty years. He then went on to praise the forthcoming appointment of Arthur Frank Bound as the Signal and Telegraph Engineer of the LMS Railway – again the article is reproduced here. (Photographs of Duffield Junction signal box appeared in *Midland Record* No. 2.)

There had recently been two railway accidents involving passenger trains at Charfield (13th October 1928) and Ashchurch (8th January 1929) when a total of twenty-one people lost their lives. Both these accidents occurred in the Crewe Division of the LMS for which Morgan was Signalling Assistant to the Divisional Civil Engineer and for which Morgan was responsible for the maintenance, which was doubtless a contributory factor in Moore's contribution to the *John Blunt* newspaper.

On 20th May 1929 Mr. A. F. Bound, who was then the Signalling Engineer of the Southern area of the LNER, was appointed S&T engineer of the LMS, and Sadler remembers on the day that Bound's appointment was announced he was attending a meeting of the IRSE in London, when at tea, Bound and Morgan came over and sat at Sadler's table, all this on the day one of Moore's articles appeared.

Sadler was surprised to see that Morgan was not in the slightest bit upset over the position and they actually began to discuss it. It so happened that Sadler had a copy of *John Blunt* containing Moore's article and naturally Bound was interested to see it. On congratulating Bound on his appointment as S&T Engineer, he enquired if Bound would like it. Bound accepted the copy and as far as is known, there the matter ended.

His leaving present, subscribed for by the staff at Derby, was a typewriter with which he said he would record his experiences. Unfortunately, these experiences were published in the *John Blunt* magazine in the way already described and in a way which no-one could foresee. On his retirement, Moore, according to the IRSE membership list, was living at 205 Drewry Lane, Derby, before moving to Somerset in 1932/3. He is understood to have bought or rented an off-licence and grocers shop on the Uttoxeter Road, Derby, not far from Drewry Lane, until he moved to Congresbury in Somerset, where he died on 22nd February 1950, being cremated in Arnos Vale Cemetery, Bristol, three days later.

There ends the interesting story of James Samuel Moore, who, at the end of a brilliant career, retired a disillusioned man – a tale which did not do the signal staff at Derby any good, and giving an insight into the relationships within the Derby Signal Dept.

Acknowledgments
John Sadler
Tony Overton
Institution of Railway Signal
   Engineers

The front page of the John Blunt *newspaper, showing the headline of Moore's article on 'Our Death-Trap Railways', also the picture of Horatio Bottomley and the two slogans, 'Tribune of the Man-in-the-Street' and 'Champion of the Bottom Dog', indicating the paper's* raison d'être.

OUR DEATH-TRAP RAILWAYS.

Amazing Revelations of Unremedied Signal Defects—What the Trial of the Charfield Engine Driver Would Have Disclosed.

AT the inquest on the victims of the Charfield railway disaster, the jury brought in a verdict of manslaughter against Driver Aldington. The Grand Jury at the Assizes very properly threw out the bill, and he was discharged.

But for this fact, evidence would have been given in open Court which would have shaken to its foundations the complacency of highly-placed railway officials.

We are in a position to reveal not only the undoubted cause of certain accidents, but the existence of grave dangers which at any moment may bring about other disasters. We are going to show that the "human element" blamed by railway directors is not the signalman nor the driver, but a far less competent, though much more highly paid, official.

A well-known railway signal engineer, with over forty years' practical experience, recently brought to the notice of the Minister of Transport a number of disturbing facts within his knowledge. His statement discloses an appalling degree of inefficiency in railway organisation and management. This engineer is Mr. J. S. Moore, a Member of the Institute of Railway Signal Engineers, and an acknowledged authority on the subject of "Interlocking."

Mr. Moore's qualifications to speak on this vital question are beyond dispute. For nineteen years he was employed by railway signalling contractors, ten of which were spent in supervising new installations on British railways. For fifteen years after that he was responsible for the signalling on the late London, Tilbury and Southend Railway, which was taken over by the Midland Company in 1912.

In 1915 Mr. Moore was transferred to the headquarters of the Midland line at Derby, as assistant to the Chief Inspector. His duties here were to draft the interlocking tables and check the locking of signals over the entire line. He says that this work had been done for fifty years previously by successive Chief Inspectors, many of whom had little or no experience in this important branch of railway engineering.

On an important line like the Midland, Mr. Moore expected to find the signalling system up to date, but was astonished to discover vital errors in the first new locking apparatus he tested—one which had been installed several months. He tested a second and a third, and found errors in each case. Subsequently he discovered **scores of defective signals, and by reference to the records was able to establish the disquieting fact that many of them had been in this state for years.**

In 1918 Mr. Moore tested a locking apparatus with 91 levers which had been installed in 1906. He found it was possible to operate some of the signals with points in conflicting positions! As a result of this discovery a new apparatus was made and erected in 1919—the Government at that time being responsible for railway shareholders' dividends, expense was therefore no object. A great many corrections were made during that period, but when the railways were decontrolled extra charges on maintenance involved awkward explanations. As a result, Mr. Moore found that his reports were not always acted upon.

In 1923 the amalgamation took place and the Midland line became part of the London, Midland and Scottish system. Early in that year, Mr. Moore was called on to investigate the cause of several derailments that had occurred at the same pair of points operated from Nottingham East Signal Box. He found that the detectors, which should have prevented either of the two signals being operated unless the points were properly closed and set for the route required, were wrongly fitted.

The following November, at Whitehall Junction, Leeds—a very important centre—it was found that two conflicting signals could be operated together, so that it had been possible for a collision to occur on the main line for fifteen years past!

Two years later Mr. Moore was retired, having reached the earliest age limit at which retirement on pension was possible.

After reading the account of the disastrous collision between two trains at Ashchurch on January 8 last, Mr. Moore referred to his notes on signalling defects. He found that he had reported a defective signal at the Gloucester end of Ashchurch Junction station on several occasions, the last report being dated June 24, 1924. This defect was, however, still in existence as lately as August, 1925, and it had then been unremedied for at least forty years—a veritable death-trap! Had the collision taken place at this end of the station, the consequences might have been even worse than they were.

Mr. Moore asserts that some of the evidence given at the Charfield Disaster Inquiry was incorrect, and he was prepared to depose as an expert witness to that effect had Driver Aldington gone to trial. He holds that many accidents that in the past have been attributed to gross negligence on the part of drivers and signalmen were really due to defective signalling apparatus and the inevitable "chance-your-arm" methods which result from faulty equipment and careless, incompetent supervision.

We come now to an explanation of the diagram reproduced below. It shows part of the signalling of an important main-line junction. When the signal box was renewed some years ago a number of the then existing signals were abolished

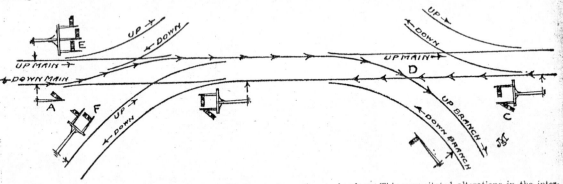

This necessitated alterations in the interlocking arrangements of the levers.

These alterations were not properly carried out, due apparently to incompetence on the part of those responsible for the work. As a result, the signals at A, E, or F may be operated with a conflicting signal at C.

Two years after the alterations had been made the signalman accepted two trains, one on the Up and the other on the Down line, operating the signals at F and C. He suddenly discovered that the trains were signalled to cross the path of each other! He replaced the signals to their "Danger" positions and averted what might have been a terrible disaster at point D.

Had a collision occurred, this signalman would probably have been blamed. The following day the locking was "corrected," but thirteen years later it was discovered that it was possible to operate signal A with a conflicting signal at C, as shown on the diagram.

It was argued at one Inquiry recently that the chances of an accident occurring through defective signals were one in a million. This may be true.

The fact, however, remains that the human operator is being depended on to make up for faults in a mechanical system which properly adjusted should be practically fool-proof.

MURDER ON THE LINE!

Daily Deadly Danger Remedied After Forty Years—L., M. and S. Moving After Our Exposure.

IT was unfortunate for the London, Midland & Scottish Railway Company that the publication of the expo re entitled "Our Death-Trap Railways " in our issue of February 16 should coincide with another lamentable accident near Doo Hill Station, East Derbyshire. The disaster was due to an "up" goods train travelling on the wrong line and colliding with a "down" express passenger train. An Inquiry is being held into the cause of the accident—*in private!*

The further diagram we now reproduce is of part of the signalling system at Duffield Station, near Derby. It shows that a similar collision might have occurred at this place at any time during the forty years over which the defects existed unremedied.

Seven years after the signal box and the interlocking apparatus had been renewed at Duffield Station, Mr. J. S. Moore, the retired signalling engineer to whom reference was made in our previous article, found that the

We are credibly informed that for many years the practice when renewing an interlocking apparatus has been to base the new locking on the original interlocking table, with little or no rega d to changes which might have taken place or to defects which existed through errors made when the signals were first installed.

R ferring again for a moment to the diagram, up-to-date interlocking requires points "C," "E," "L," and "D" to be operated before Signal "O," and Points "A," "F," "I," "E," "L,"

ling and unprecedented series of accidents has been needed to wake up a great railway company to its responsibilities in this direction.

Inefficiency in this respect reflects itself in every other department of railway administration and management.

The safety and comfort of the travelling public and the important services demanded by industry and commerce have been subordinated to a frantic desire to make profits. That viewpoint has been entirely wrong. Had efficiency

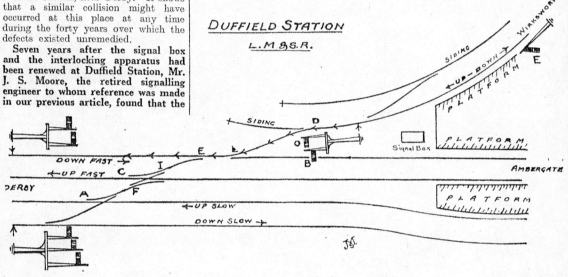

DUFFIELD STATION
L. M & S. R.

"up" branch home signal "E" shown on the diagram could be lowered to the "All right" position with the points "L" and "D" set for the down fast train line!

Forty years ago, when the number of trains passing daily over any given track was comparatively few, an elementary system of signalling was safe enough, and the intervening signals at "O" and "B" afforded sufficient security. Unfortunately, intervening signals are sometimes passed at "danger," and an "up" train could pass on to the "down" fast train line with the possibility of meeting a "down" express in a head-on collision.

It is appalling to realise that such a primitive system of signalling has been allowed to stand all through the years that railway traffic has continuously increased in volume. The fact that interlocking devices have been perfected so that it may be made impossible for two trains to meet, renders the negligence to apply the system properly all the more deplorable. The trouble has been that the officials responsible have been incompetent, and those above them who should have been able to check their work have been unable to do so through sheer ignorance.

and "D" before Signal "B." Signal "E" is locked in its "danger" position when points "L" and "D" are as shown, until signal "O" or "B" is operated to the "All right" position. This may be somewhat difficult for the lay reader to follow, but it will be understood, at any rate, that with a proper system of interlocking in force, there can be no collisions or accidents unless the engine driver deliberately ignores the signals—a thing which, of course, no sane employee ever does.

Signs are not lacking that the London, Midland & Scottish Railway Company are alive to the position.

Within the last few days the appointment has been announced of Mr. A. S. Bound, Signal and Telegraph Engineer of the Southern Area of the London and North Eastern Railway, as Signal and Telegraph Engineer to the L., M. and S.

In these days of fast moving traffic and highly complicated junctions where masses of railway lines intersect, signalling systems cannot be simple. Their installation and maintenance requires the best brains of the railway engineering world. That they have r.ot had them in every case is painfully evident. It is an unpleasant reflection that an appal-

been placed first, the financial reward would have followed as surely as day follows night.

To declare that it is safer to travel by rail than by road will not increase the passenger receipts on any railway. The traveller is not greatly concerned with statistics. He would rather take a chance of a toss from a motor-car into a hedge than commit himself to the mercy of an express train, knowing that an obsolete signalling system is making him the sport of chance with the ever-present prospect of a hideous death.

One more point of great significance may be noted.

On all the railway lines that have been electrified accidents are exceptionally rare, even at bottle-neck termini with their mazes of transversing points. There is evidence of a thoroughly efficient system of control. Why cannot an equally good system be installed on all other lines?

The cowardly evasion of responsibility that blames the "human element" is a gross insult to our engine drivers and signalmen—conscientious and hardworking bodies of men none too well paid for the perilous and important duties they carry out so well.

Extract from the **John Blunt** *newspaper dated 2nd March 1929 with the article 'Murder on the Line'.*

The original c.1879 picture of Thurgarton station, looking towards Nottingham, with the Kind family, as described in the article, on the station platform.
CTY. KIND FAMILY

An enlargement from the Thurgarton photograph to show a Midland Railway single-wheeled barrow loaded with a packing case and a travelling trunk. In common with all Midland platform barrows, they were constructed by the Carriage and Wagon Department at Derby and, although not clearly visible, the side frame had painted on it the letters 'M.R.' followed by a number. From photographic evidence, they were not as numerous as the two-wheeled variety and were mostly confined to stations of lesser importance. These barrows appear to have all gone by the end of the 1930s, but it would be interesting to know if any survived into the next decade. Presumably they were not replaced when worn out, the two-wheeled barrow being considered more suitable for traffic purposes, as a single-wheeled barrow tended to tip sideways if unevenly loaded. This was unavoidable in certain circumstances, whereas a two-wheeled barrow remained relatively stable.

Thurgarton Station

with a note on MR single-wheeled barrows

by JIM JACKSON

This picture of Thurgarton station was taken facing north-east towards Lincoln. According to a note on the reverse of the picture, the date was c.1906. The locomotive, a Johnson 2–4–0, was carrying a smokebox numberplate and the signalbox appears to be the 1902 box.

COLLECTION R. J. ESSERY

Thurgarton Station is situated on the Nottingham—Lincoln branch, some 9¾ miles from Nottingham. The original of the accompanying photograph, taken in about 1879, is in the possession of the family of the late Arthur Kind and presents several early Midland Railway features that are worthy of study.

Beyond the level crossing gates we can see the first Thurgarton signal box, which was replaced in 1902. The group of men standing on the platform at the far end appear to be platelayers, three of whom were holding a heavy hand roller. One of its uses may have been to roll and keep level the unmetalled platform surface. The inside-keyed track in front of the platform was ballasted above sleeper level whilst the early pattern of lamp and post on the right, most certainly oil lit, probably pre-dated the MR hexagonal post design. A single-wheeled platform barrow can also be seen in the centre, flanked by two uniformed railwaymen. To the right of the platform barrow, the station master, John Kind, is pictured with his wife and six of their children who were, from left to right, John Alfred, born 1.9.1865; Herbert Henry, born 8.4.1867; Samuel Charles (in mother's arms), born 18.7.1876; Frederick William, born 16.4.1870; Arthur Edwin, born 18.2.1872; and Albert Ernest, born 27.2.1874.

Arthur Edwin Kind followed in his father's footsteps, eventually becoming station master at Collingham in 1900, a position he held for over 30 years until his retirement in 1932. Arthur Kind was held in high esteem, a member of the local Methodist Church and a man who put his religious principles into practice. Of him it was said that he was 'Kind by name and kind by nature'.

Today Thurgarton station building is in private ownership, the furthest bay having been removed and replaced with a new window and plain wall. Otherwise the building is little altered, even retaining its Midland pattern bargeboard. On 8th

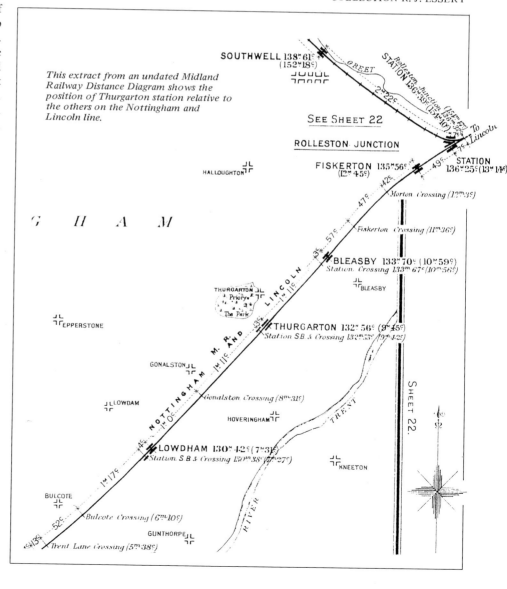

This extract from an undated Midland Railway Distance Diagram shows the position of Thurgarton station relative to the others on the Nottingham and Lincoln line.

This 11th May 1968 view of the station building should be compared with the c.1906 picture; note the changes that had been made to the building. The most obvious are the replacement chimney pots and the new chimney to the rear and the removal of the lamps. D. F. TEE

March 1982 a number of alterations were made at Thurgarton and were described in Weekly Operating Notice LM10 for 1982 from which the following are noted. A new up platform, situated on the Nottingham side of the level crossing was brought into use, replacing the former up platform situated on the Lincoln side of the level crossing. At the same time, the crossing box, together with all signals worked therefrom, was taken away. The crossing was converted to an 'open' type, having steady-amber/flashing-red road traffic signals, together with 'Another train coming' signs, but having neither gates nor barriers. Appertaining to the railway, flashing white lights were provided, situated 5 yards before reaching the crossing, with advance warning boards, 1,464 yards on the Lowdham side of the crossing and 1,442 yards on the Fiskerton side. A permanent speed restriction of 55mph for passenger trains and 35mph for goods trains was introduced.

The above level crossing arrangements were not entirely satisfactory and, following several incidents involving lorries carrying sand and gravel from the nearby Hoveringham gravel pits, the level crossing was provided with half barriers on Sunday, 12th June 1988. This was recorded in the Weekly Operating Notice No. LM11 for 1988 as follows:

'The existing Automatic Open Crossing Locally Monitored (AOCL) will be converted to an Automatic Half Barrier Crossing (AHB).

'The 55mph permanent speed restriction for passenger trains and 35mph for freight trains which apply between the Down and Up lines between the speed restriction boards and the crossing will be removed. The advance warning boards, differential speed restriction boards and drivers' flashing white lights will be recovered.'

The accompanying photographs were taken after the 1982 alterations but before the installation of the half barriers.

Acknowledgements
The writer is indebted to the family of the late Arthur Kind for the loan of the original photograph and for supplying family details.

Station Clocks

Notes by BOB ESSERY

Recently, when going through my files, I came across these photographs of station clocks taken by the late Malcolm Cross. Two were taken at Bedford and the other at Trent, but unfortunately no dates were given. I have used Malcolm's rather sparse notes for the caption and wonder if any reader can throw further light on the subject.

My first meeting with Malcolm would have been at Central Hall during the 1960s where his model railway was exhibited. During the years that followed, we shared a common interest in the Midland Railway and a number of contributions from him have been published in *Midland Record*.

This interesting artefact was erected on the Down platform waiting room wall at Bedford. It had a triangular aspect, with two faces toward the platform and another inside the waiting room. A BR official kindly opened the casing of the clock for the photograph to be taken. The width of the wall on which it was mounted was 3ft. Both clock dials appear to be of BR (LM) origin.

Station clock at Trent. A similar clock was provided at Buxton, which had a 2ft 6in diameter face and the wooden base on which it was mounted measured 6ft 2in x 19in x 5½in thick.

Other than to suggest this picture was taken during the 1930s, it has not been possible to give a precise date. The express passenger train hauled by M&GNR 4—4—0 No. 56 was photographed as the train was approaching Nottingham and reference to the Company's Working Time Table provides some interesting information. In the 11th July 1927 table there is a section headed 'Joint Trains working over other companies' lines'. This shows a passenger train that departed from Bourne at 4.26 p.m., arriving at Nottingham at 5.40 p.m. The return working was given as 'depart from Nottingham at 7.25 p.m. arrive at Bourne at 4.26 p.m.' This would allow time for the engine to be prepared for the return working. My copy of the 11th September 1933 table gives two Saturday-only arrivals at Nottingham, one at 2.40 p.m., the other at 3.15 p.m. There was also a weekday arrival at 5.40 p.m. Departures from Nottingham for the Joint line were at 4.17 p.m. and 7.30 p.m., both trains running throughout the week. During the 1930s there was a considerable amount of through Saturday-only summer working between Yarmouth and Lowestoft and the Midlands that was handled by these elderly 4—4—0s. The subject of train services to and from the Midland by M&GNR trains is not one that appears to have commanded much attention, and after reading the timetable, it seemed to me that this is an area where further research is required. Turning now to the locomotive, I can say No. 56 was one of forty locomotives that were designed at Derby and built for the Joint line between 1894 and 1899, this example being constructed by Sharp Stewart in 1896. It was rebuilt with a G7 Belpaire boiler as shown here in 1912 and was in this condition when in 1936 the M&GNR locomotive stock was transferred to the LNER. The locomotive was renumbered 056 in February 1937 and was withdrawn from service in November 1943.

T. G. HEPBURN

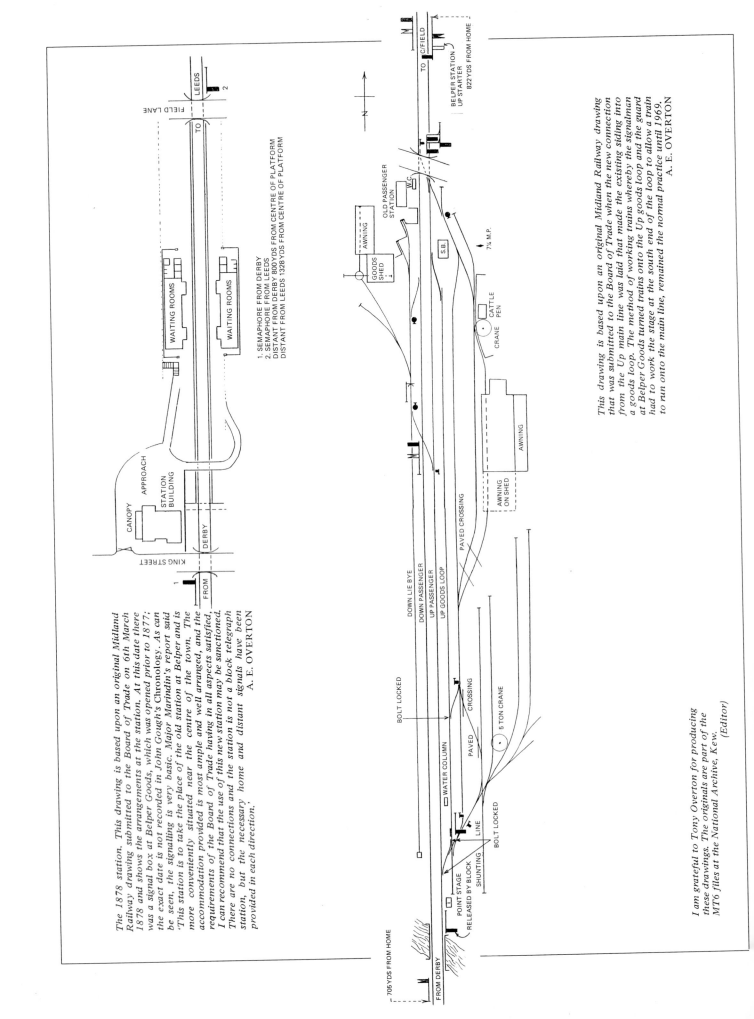

TO LEEDS

FIELD LANE

TO

2

WAITING ROOMS

WAITING ROOMS

1. SEMAPHORE FROM DERBY
2. SEMAPHORE FROM LEEDS
DISTANT FROM DERBY 800 YDS FROM CENTRE OF PLATFORM
DISTANT FROM LEEDS 1328 YDS FROM CENTRE OF PLATFORM

APPROACH

STATION BUILDING

CANOPY

KING STREET

DERBY

FROM

1

The 1878 station. This drawing is based upon an original Midland Railway drawing submitted to the Board of Trade on 6th March 1878 and shows the arrangements at the station. At this date there was a signal box at Belper Goods, which was opened prior to 1877; the exact date is not recorded in John Gough's Chronology. As can be seen, the signalling is very basic. Major Marindin's report said 'This station is to take the place of the old station at Belper and is more conveniently situated near the centre of the town. The accommodation provided is most ample and well arranged, and the requirements of the Board of Trade having in all aspects satisfied, I can recommend that the use of this new station may be sanctioned. There are no connections and the station is not a block telegraph station, but the necessary home and distant signals have been provided in each direction.'
A. E. OVERTON

TO C/FIELD

BELPER STATION
UP STARTER

822 YDS FROM HOME

OLD PASSENGER STATION

AWNING

W.C.

GOODS SHED

S.B.

7¼ M.P.

CRANE

CATTLE PEN

AWNING

AWNING ON SHED

PAVED CROSSING

DOWN LIE BYE

DOWN PASSENGER

UP PASSENGER

UP GOODS LOOP

BOLT LOCKED

CROSSING

5 TON CRANE

WATER COLUMN

PAVED

LINE

POINT STAGE
RELEASED BY BLOCK

SHUNTING

BOLT LOCKED

BOLT LOCKED

705 YDS FROM HOME

FROM DERBY

This drawing is based upon an original Midland Railway drawing that was submitted to the Board of Trade when the new connection from the Up main line was laid that made the existing siding into a goods loop. The method of working trains whereby the signalman at Belper Goods turned trains onto the Up goods loop and the guard had to work the stage at the south end of the loop to allow a train to run onto the main line, remained the normal practice until 1969.
A. E. OVERTON

I am grateful to Tony Overton for producing these drawings. The originals are part of the MT6 files at the National Archive, Kew.
(Editor)

BELPER STATION

Notes by BOB ESSERY

Looking north towards Leeds, this picture was taken from the footbridge. This connected the footpaths from the platforms to the approach and the station buildings that fronted onto Kings Street. According to the Derby photograph register, this picture was taken in November 1911. Note the positions of the milk churns, which may have been placed in anticipation of where they were to be loaded in the train. When set formations of rolling stock were used and providing the driver stopped the train at the same place each time, it was possible to ensure that traffic to be loaded was to hand and not some distance away on the platform. Above all, this picture demonstrates the value of a sighting board behind a signal arm.
NATIONAL RAILWAY MUSEUM (DY2459)

The North Midland Railway was one of the three railway companies that, by amalgamation, formed the Midland Railway on 10th May 1844. The line from Derby to Masborough was opened on 11th May 1840 with the first Belper station opening on the same date. This remained in use until the new passenger station at King Street was opened on 10th March 1878. Some years ago, the late Peter Turville, who lived close to Belper, gave me a picture of the station and the OS map reproduced in this article, suggesting that one day I could use them in *Midland Record*. Sadly, he did not live to see his gift in print.

The accompanying extract from the 1920 edition of the Midland Railway Distance Diagram shows that Belper goods station was 134 miles 79 chains from St. Pancras and the passenger station 34 chains further north. In the close vicinity of Belper the railway crossed the River Derwent three times and the diagram also shows the Up goods line that was opened on 6th October 1912.

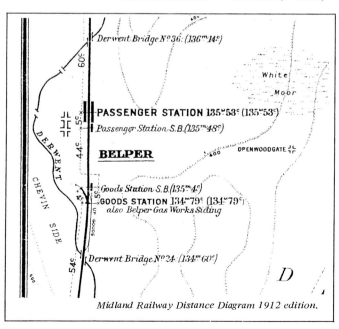

Midland Railway Distance Diagram 1912 edition.

A similar view taken on the same day, showing the approach roads to both platforms and the stop signal in the clear position. Note the number of gas lamps on each platform; there can be little doubt that this station was well illuminated.

NATIONAL RAILWAY MUSEUM (DY2458)

PASSENGERS
MUST CROSS
THE LINE BY
THE BRIDGE

LADIES
ROOM

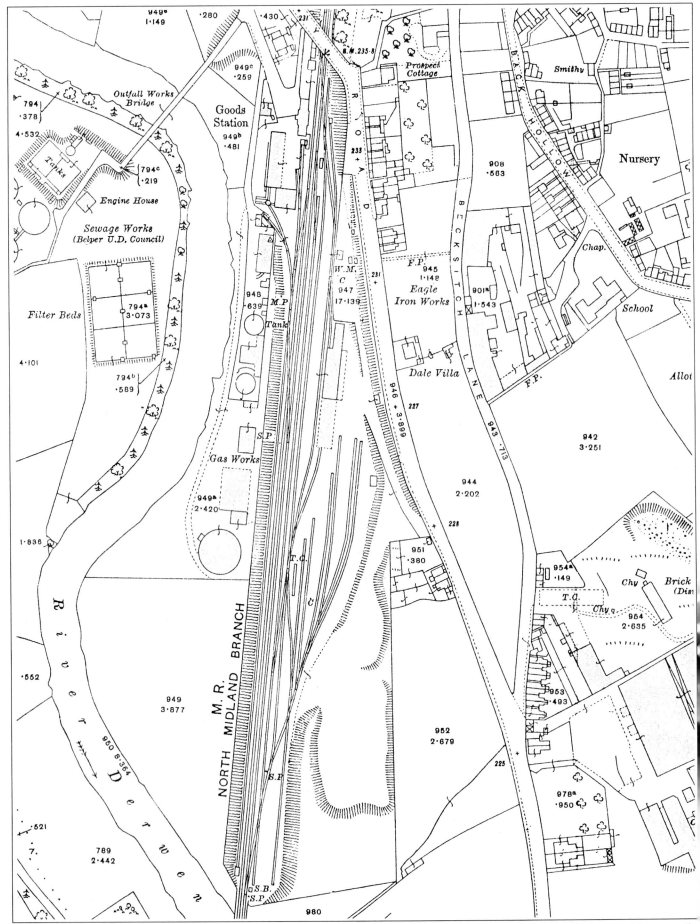

Taken from 25-inch Ordnance Survey of 1914. (Crown copyright reserved)

This is another view taken from the footbridge. The Down passenger train was headed by an unidentified 2–4–0 and appears to have consisted of five clerestory carriages with an arc-roof vehicle the second from the engine. Note the milk churns were in a similar position to those seen in the previous pictures. COLLECTION R. J. ESSERY

This is a similar view except that the photographer had moved to the left in order to get a better view of the train. The date of the picture is c.1890-96 and the locomotive, a '1070' class 2–4–0, is seen with a mixture of bogie and six-wheel Clayton arc-roof carriages with what appears to have been a four-wheel passenger brake van at the rear of the train. COLLECTION R. J. ESSERY

Ex Midland Compound No. 1005 at the head of an Up express passenger train on 4th May 1934. This picture also shows the old Midland Railway station nameboard on the Up platform.

H. C. CASSERLEY

This south-facing picture shows the footbridge that connected the up and down platforms via the footpaths. Just visible to the right, behind the telegraph poles, the rear of the station building can be seen.

D. IBBOTSON

This picture was taken at the north end of the station c.1967 and shows the retaining walls with the various bridges towards Broadholme.

D. IBBOTSON

The Midland Railway photograph register describes this picture as 'New Viaduct, Swainsley, Belper', but no date is given. The OS map shows Swainsley as being on the west side of the River Derwent, shown as Bridge No. 24 on the Distance Diagram, and this is confirmed by the buffer stop at the end of the Up goods Loop which can be seen on the right of the picture. The Midland painting style of Denby pottery cream and Venetian red (chocolate) can be clearly seen. NATIONAL RAILWAY MUSEUM (DY3998)

By the way...
Miscellaneous observations concerning previous issues

MIDLAND RECORD No. 15

On page 9 of *Midland Record* No. 15, the caption states that the fire at Somers Town was c.1905, but the following extract from *The Times* dated Monday 29th June 1903, page 8, col. 4, gives an account of the fire which had occurred the previous night.

'FIRE AT THE MIDLAND RAILWAY GOODS WAREHOUSE
For several hours last night a large force of the London firemen was actively engaged in coping with a fire which broke out shortly before 6 o'clock in the top floor of one of the goods warehouses of the Midland Railway Company in St. Pancras Road, Somers Town. The fire was first discovered in a building six floors high, extending about 100 yards in one direction and having a width of nearly 30 yards, which was closely stored with merchandise of every description. A force of 25 steamers, two long ladders, three horsed escapes, and 150 firemen concentrated at the scene under Captain Wells, the chief officer, and Mr. S. G. Gamble, the second officer. A numerous body of the London Salvage Corps, directed by Colonel Fox, also gathered to render assistance. At half-past 6 o'clock the top floor was blazing from end to end, and the fire, running down the lift shaft, had involved the floors beneath. Fanned by a light westerly breeze, the fire gained increased strength every minute, and for a couple of hours the firemen worked with visible effect. The Salvage Corps men succeeded in pulling out tons of valuable goods from the lower floors and removing them to a safe place; none the less, great damage was caused to the remainder. About half-past 8 o'clock it was found possible to circulate the official 'stop' message as follows:— "Stop for the Midland Railway Company's goods yard; it has been a burn-out of three floors and roof destroyed." The work of the firemen was by no means at an end, however, and fresh men were ordered on at 9 o'clock at night.'

Tony Overton
Nottingham

MIDLAND RECORD No. 21

The photo on page 34 is in fact at the Signal Works, specifically the part located in the Derby North Junction/Derby South Junction triangle, and looking north. The round-roofed building to the rear of the tank bears a sign indicating it is Smiths Shop No. 2 — the building in the left background was also a Smiths Shop, and there was another in the original portion of the works on the west side of the Derby–Sheffield line. To the right is the Box Shop (nearest bit) and the Post Shop (furthest bit), while the structure on the extreme left was, I believe, the Paint Shop. At least two of the buildings display 'Do Not Spit' signs — an attempt to avoid the spread of tuberculosis as I understand it.

Pure speculation, but I wonder — given the March 1915 date — if the tank shown was put in as a static water tank for fire-fighting purposes? Both the Locomotive Works and the Carriage & Wagon Works were bombed by Zeppelins in February 1916, so this may have been a precautionary measure. Certainly, most of the buildings in this part of the Signal Works were of timber.

Mark Higginson
The Silk Mill, Derby's Museum of Industry & History

MIDLAND RECORD No. 24

In the article 'The Longbridge and Halesowen Joint Line', on page 65, the caption with the photograph of a single line train staff instrument states that the instrument is a Webb-Thompson staff machine. I am afraid this is wrong; the machine or 'instrument' in the photograph is a Railway Signal Company 'miniature' Train Staff instrument. The Webb-Thompson Train Staff machine was an L&NWR patented invention and manufactured both by that company and also under licence by the Railway Signal Company of Fazakerley, Liverpool. Being over 4ft tall, they stood on the floor and its single line train staffs were about 3ft long.

The disadvantage of Webb-Thompson train staffs was that they were cumbersome to handle and therefore awkward to exchange with a train travelling at speed. To get around this the R.S. Co. introduced its own 'miniature' train staff instrument during 1906. This new instrument stood about 2ft 4in tall and could be mounted on a shelf or cupboard top, and the staffs used in the instrument were slim and only 10¾in long.

Railway Signal Co. 'miniature' Train Staff instruments were widely used in Ireland but none are known to have been installed by any pre-grouping companies in the UK. However, during the 1920s and 30s, the LMS replaced a number of Webb-Thompson instruments on its single lines with R.S. Co. 'miniature' Train Staff instruments.

We regret we have mislaid the name of the writer of this letter.

Regarding bridge plates (pages 86-91), bridge numbers were 'writ on tablets of stone' and were, so far as I am aware, never altered during the lifetime of the bridge; hence the comment on the drawings 'The existing bridge and culvert numbers are not to be altered . . . '

If a bridge was demolished, the number remained vacant and any new bridges were allocated the number of the previous bridge plus a letter suffix.

I assume the numbers first appeared on the original land plans but not on the deposited plans with the Parliamentary Bill.

I am not sure whether this still applies as the current bridge plates also have a line reference, e.g. at Keighley this is TJC = Tapton Junction Colne plus the bridge number. The number may, of course, still be the original.

John Edgington
York

Regarding the gale of 14th/15th October 1881 mentioned on page 4, you may be interested in the following extracts from the LNWR Minutes on a similar theme. These are the only references that I can find. The LNWR did not note the gale of October 1881 and the Midland did not appear to note those mentioned in the LNWR Minutes.

LNWR Locomotive Committee Minutes, February 1883
Springs Branch. The new signal box in course of erection at Springs Branch was blown [down] during the heavy gale on the morning of 26th January. . . . . During the same gale 6 signal posts were blown down and 55 signal arms blown off. As there are a large number of arms blown off during every gale Mr. Webb has arranged to make those for the new pattern posts of corrugated steel which should withstand the heaviest gale without breakage.

LNWR Locomotive Committee Minutes, January 1884
5 signals were blown down and 187 arms blown off during the gale of 11th and 12th December 1883.

LNWR Locomotive Committee Minutes, January 1895
During the course of the severe gale of 22nd December 1894, 99 wood signal arms were blown away, and 53 steel arms bent or otherwise damaged, and four small signal posts were blown away.

Philip A. Millard
Woking

The note on page 69 of Don Powell's recollections about train staff working — 'a small token instrument to Longbridge East signalbox when West box was switched out' — might be confusing. This is compounded by the fact that the table of train staff working on page 31 of MR No. 23 omitted the footnote that accompanies the dagger mark. The footnote reads 'When Longbridge West signalbox is closed, the line between Rubery and Longbridge East is worked by token, the shape being round and colour red, and is treated as a long section token'.

The LMS appendix used the word 'token' to cover both electric train staffs (ETS) and key tokens. Normally a long section token applies to the length of line worked by two short section tokens. That did not apply here, because there was no short section token from Longbridge West to Longbridge East. When West signalbox was open, the working between those two boxes was double line worked by absolute block.

In summary, the working was
Halesowen to Rubery, Large ETS, configuration B
Rubery to Longbridge West, Large ETS, configuration A
Rubery to Longbridge East with West box switched out, Miniature ETS, 'S' pattern, configuration A
So the driver and signalman exchanging staffs in the photograph on page 66 of MR No. 24 are exchanging large staffs, because Longbridge West was switched in.

The miniature staff instrument at Rubery shown in the photo on page 65 is the long section staff instrument to Longbridge East.

The captions to the photos on page 69 have been reversed. It is the lower photo that shows 'Contractor's Siding' ground frame (that is the name shown in the Sectional Appendix) — the hut with the curved roof — that worked the points to the sidings seen beyond. These points were too far from the signalbox to be worked directly. The ground frame, within the protection of fixed signals, was bolt locked (released) from the signalbox (lever 12). Neither photograph on page 69 shows the Frogmill Ground Frame.

The disused signal fittings on the signal post on page 69 appear to have been for
a) The arm below the remaining arm — a distant signal for Frogmill Crossing, later replaced by Frogmill having control of the Up Starting signal through slotting
b) The arm facing trains approaching Rubery (at top of post) had a Down direction Outer Home signal. There was latterly a spare lever in the signalbox, where the sequence of down line signal levers was
14 Down Starter
15 Down Home
16 Spare
17 Down Distant, slotted by Frogmill Crossing

The arrangements of the double distant signal at Frogmill were unusual in having two distant signal arms on one post. Even more unusual was the fact that the top arm did not refer to the level crossing (which an approaching train would encounter first). So, since the distant arm for the signalbox was seldom operated, the aspect that drivers normally saw was yellow over green — the reverse of the normal green over yellow aspect.

The photographs enclosed show a typical Blasting Staff. This one was for the Skipton Rock Co. These staffs were not usually interlocked with the signalling, and the example shown is of a size and shape that suggests that it was made from a standard brake stick, with the lettering deeply engraved into the wood.

M. Christensen
Leamington Spa

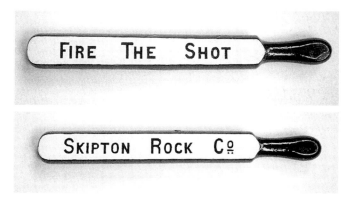

In the article 'The Midland Railway's early access to London', I was rather intrigued by the maps showing a Midland Railway station and a 'Midland Counties' engine shed in the middle of the Great Northern Railway's goods depot.

However, the Midland did not start running its own trains to London upon the opening of the Leicester & Hitchin line in 1857, as the 1853 Act for this line only gave permission for the Midland to make a junction with the Great Northern Railway at Hitchin. The Act did oblige the Midland, however, 'to provide a reasonable number of trains daily to meet the trains of the Great Northern Railway'. In other words, the operation at Hitchin was to be similar to that at Rugby with the Midland handing over its traffic to another company for forwarding to London.

Running powers were not generally granted by Act of Parliament (are there any examples of this?) but by agreement between the companies concerned. This was usually when there were clear benefits to both parties, or as part of the price paid to persuade another company to abandon a proposed line. An example of this was in 1866 when the Midland obtained running powers in perpetuity from Barnsley to Huddersfield via Penistone over the Manchester, Sheffield & Lincolnshire and Lancashire & Yorkshire railways. In return, the Midland agreed to drop its bill then in the House of Lords for a new line from Barnsley to Kirkburton.

The situation with the Great Northern was somewhat different, as running powers were not granted in perpetuity and it became increasingly difficult to conclude that both parties benefited from the agreement.

The first agreement was made with the Great Northern Railway on 5th May 1857. This allowed the Midland the use of Hitchin station at a cost of £500 per annum. The second agreement was dated 1st June 1858 and gave the Midland access to the line from Hitchin to London including full use of King's Cross passenger station and to all the goods stations from Holloway to King's Cross. The Midland was also allowed to open a ticket office and a parcels office in the Great Northern station and the only restriction was to bar the Midland from taking traffic from any station between London and Hitchin. The agreement could be terminated at seven years notice by either company.

In the light of this and the fact that the passenger timetables refer to 'London King's Cross', it would appear that the Midland regular passenger services used the main Great Northern from 1858 to 1868.

What then of the 'Midland Station' in the goods yard? The commentary to the Alan Godfrey reprint of the 1870 map of the area notes that the 'Maiden Lane' (the old name for York Road) terminus of the Great Northern, prior to the opening of King's Cross in 1852, became the potato market. But Jack Simmons, in his *The Railway in Town and Country, 1830-1913* (pp. 49-50) states that the potato market was first held in the goods station and then in 1864 moved to a new building at a cost of £40,000. I think therefore that the building marked 'Midland Station' was the original Maiden Lane station of 1850. There is also the reference, as noted in the article, to Alan Jackson's book *London Termini* where it states that many Midland excursion trains for the Great International Exhibition in 1862 were accommodated in the Goods Yard. Perhaps this was the reason for the appellation on the map.

The north/west branch from the Great Northern to the North London line was authorised by a Great Northern Act of 1859. I do not know why it should be referred to as the 'Midland Branch' on the map.

Finally, it is interesting to compare the Midland's efforts to reach London with that of the Great Central Railway. Both sought to avoid the expense of driving a line through the Chilterns and so connected with existing lines north of the escarpment. Both had rather stormy relations with their erstwhile partners and ended up constructing independent lines.

NOTES
1. The agreements for running powers are attached as schedules to Midland Acts of Parliament, the Barnsley to Kirkburton to the Act

of 1866, and the agreements with the Great Northern Railway to the London Station Act of 1860.
2. The annual cost of the running powers over the Great Northern to London was rather complicated, being made up of:
   • £1,500 for the use of King's Cross station
   • 6% of the capital cost of the engine shed, plus any maintenance and repairs
   • Gas and water consumed
   • 1/9d per ton of coal or coke carried
   • 2d for coke and 1/- for coal carried for the use of locomotives
   • For other traffic to/from non-competitive locations within 64 miles from London (approximately Irchester), a mileage rate set by the Great Northern Railway
   • For other traffic to/from non-competitive locations greater than 64 miles from London, based on mileage rates charged by the Midland Railway
   • For other traffic to competitive locations, a mileage rate charged at the greater of the Midland and the Great Northern rates
   • There was a minimum payment of £20,000 for charges based on traffic carried.
3. A detailed track layout of the original St. Pancras Goods Yard is reproduced in E. G. Barnes' *The Rise of the Midland Railway 1844-1874*, pp. 216-7 from the parliamentary plans to the 1865 New Lines and Additional Powers Act.
4. Jack Simmons gives as his reference the chairman's speech of 3rd August in R1110/172.

Andrew Surry
Hitchin

In *Midland Record* No. 24, we featured the goods station at Queen's Road, Sheffield and on page 82 I said that although we were able to show two of the three pictures that were taken by the Midland Railway photographer, it would be helpful if we could illustrate the rest of the depot. Reader Chris Crofts came to the rescue and supplied the missing print. The Derby negative number would be 12673 but his copy came from the National Archive at Kew. I am most grateful to him for making this available. There is an interesting mixture of vehicles to be seen, for example the Midland Railway Refrigerator Meat Vans. What I find most interesting is the timber on the ground (see page 82/83 as well as in this view) and no evidence of a mobile crane. Maybe some reader can comment further. *(Editor)*